THREE STEPS TO WEALTH AND POWER

Unleash Your Potential for Unlimited Achievement

By

Christopher Howard

THREE STEPS TO WEALTH AND POWER

Unleash Your Potential for Unlimited Achievement

This book was originally published by
The Christopher Howard Companies
1601 North Sepulveda Blvd. #395
Manhattan Beach, California 90266
in conjunction with Universal Events Inc.
118 Alfred St., Milsons Point NSW, Australia 2061

ISBN D-9749029-1-8

Printed in Los Angeles, California and Sydney, Australia
First Edition: February 2004
Second Edition: June 2004

Cover Design by Loren Myers
Cover Photo by Erik Arniston
Illustrations by Christine Winters

Contents

STEP ONE
WAKE UP!

ONE	Wake Up to Possibility!	15
TWO	The Playing Field of Life	19
THREE	Focus	27
FOUR	The Rules of the Game	39
FIVE	What Rules Are You Playing By?	65

STEP TWO
CHOOSE YOUR GAME

SIX	Model the Change You Want to Be	77
SEVEN	Install Excellence in Yourself Through Speed Modeling™ —What To Do	85
EIGHT	How To Do It	105

STEP THREE
PLAY TO WIN!

NINE	Play to Win—An Introduction	131
TEN	Your Road Map to Success: Vision, Mission, Goals and Values	137
ELEVEN	The Success Formula of Masters	159
TWELVE	Who's on My Team?	165
THIRTEEN	The Power of Rapport	171
FOURTEEN	Values—The Key to Influence and Inspiration	185
FIFTEEN	Win-Win Sales and Negotiation	199
SIXTEEN	How to Communicate with Power	227
SEVENTEEN	The Art of Spin and Masterful Story Telling	233
EIGHTEEN	Golden Rules for Success	255
NINTEEN	Conclusion: The One Thing That Can Change Everything	267

Appendix	271
Bibliography	289
Index	293

Michael—this one's for you.

ACKNOWLEDGEMENTS

As I say in this book, the best way to carry out any grand vision is by pulling together a great team that helps you take it to that next level and make it happen. *Three Steps to Wealth and Power* is a perfect demonstration of that concept in action. It could not have come together in the time that it did without the dedication and hard work of my fellow teammates.

Big thanks to Karen Corban for being an outstanding partner and friend. I am eternally grateful to Wendy Beacock for being there from the very beginning and for her hard work, support, and advice along the way. To Bob and Cindy Shearin for seeing the spark and fanning the flame. To Helen and Michael Bueno for their unconditional support and Lisa Jeffers for her belief and support early on. I also wish to thank Karen McCreadie for her major contribution writing and editing, for taking a diamond in the rough and turning it into something to be admired, Aricia Lee for making it real and for her hours of writing and hard work, and Amy Sorkin for cleaning up our act. I want to acknowledge Chris and Jill Stoten for keeping the machine turning, Debbie Korte for kicking it into high gear, Christine Winters for her artistry and friendship, Renée Robinson and Joyce Uptmor for all their help along the way, and Alexi for his sizzling copywriting.

To the "Dream Team" at The Christopher Howard Companies who help so many make their dreams come true, including my own, here's to an incredible job and an incredible future! I am also indebted to all of my teachers past and present for allowing me to stand on their tall shoulders, so that I could open the doorways to my dreams and assist others to do the same.

INTRODUCTION

Many teachers throughout the years have reminded me of the concept of beginning with the end in mind. That is to say that the first step in getting what you want is to determine *what* you want. This principle holds a special significance for me as I write the introduction to this book.

Just a few short years ago I remember lying on the bed of my apartment, which was actually just a converted garage. Things were NOT working for me at the time. For one, I was struggling financially. In fact, it got so bad at one point that my gas was cut off and I was bathing with buckets of microwaved water and eating only every third day.

The most frustrating part of it all was the fact that I had read hundreds of books on personal development and had attended seminar after seminar—Tony Robbins, Robert Kiyosaki, Franklin Covey, all of whom I am indebted to for all the great information. Yet I still wasn't able to make my life work. There seemed to be something missing from the equation. I knew what to do, but not how to do it. I had "awakened the giant within" and when I woke him up, he was just as frustrated as I was that we weren't any further along in our life. I could quote verses from *Rich Dad, Poor Dad*, yet I was still a very poor kid.

I felt desperately lost and off course. Yet in my heart I knew that I was capable of much more. Perhaps as you read this you can relate to the frustration and confusion I was feeling. Have you ever felt like you could have more, be more, or accomplish more in your life? Or perhaps you just feel you should be further along than you are.

Well that's where I was and I'd finally had enough. So I started to write down huge goals for myself. I wrote furiously for hours. I wrote down all the traits and qualities I admired in others. I wrote down all the things I wanted to own. I wrote down all the experiences I wanted to have in my lifetime and all the things I wanted to do. I wrote about my childhood dreams and my ultimate career path. I didn't let any judgment enter my head. I just wrote down everything that I wanted to be part of my future, no matter how ridiculous it seemed at the time, without worrying about *how* it was going to happen.

Many of the goals seemed impossibly out of reach. Yet, they ended up paving the way toward the entirely new way of life I now enjoy.

1. I wrote that I would be speaking around the country within my lifetime. I now conduct seminars and training programs on wealth, power, and personal influence to thousands of people around the world.

2. I wrote that I would have a high-rise office on the ocean. As I write this I'm gazing out my window at a school of dolphins jumping in the water, so close it looks like I could reach out and touch them!

3. I wrote that I would be on a career path I really enjoyed. Today I get to help people break through their greatest challenges and transform their lives. I find this work exciting and motivating, and know I'm blessed to feel so passionately about my life's work.

4. I wrote that I would be making every day an epic adventure and living life to the max. Whether I am taking one of my seminar groups, hang-gliding or hot-air ballooning over the beautiful resort town of Palm Springs, I am truly living life to the fullest and I get to assist others to do the same, which is one of my greatest sources of joy.

5. I wrote that I would become a multi-millionaire. I've since gone from $70,000 in debt to building a $1.5 million dollar company in two years using the techniques presented in this book. I have now set my sights on bil-

lions, which I am currently building and creating. I don't *do it for the money as much as for the fun and challenge.* I plan to give my personal wealth back to society at the end of my life in the form of a charitable foundation.

Most of the goals that I wrote down on that red-letter day in the little converted garage have come true. I say this not to impress you but rather to impress upon you what you are capable of. How did I do it?

My immense frustration drove me to create a new system for getting inside the heads of the world's most successful people and emulating their success faster than ever before. Then I used the knowledge and tools I gained to catapult myself forward in my career and my life. The great news is that I have distilled the very best of my research and my discoveries and I am presenting them for the first time in this book as Creation Technologies™, Speed Modeling™ and Strategic Partnering™. I will share with you the science and tools that I used to literally transform every aspect of my life.

CREATION TECHNOLOGIES™

If you find you no longer enjoy life and you crave change, I guarantee you that if you read this book and apply the technologies that lie within **you will change your life**. And that's a promise.

In the early years of my career I worked with several leadership and communication companies, soaking up new knowledge, skills, and information. When I began to really seek out the best technologies available I found the cutting-edge tools of Ericksonian Hypnosis and Neuro Linguistic Programming (NLP) to be the best of the best at the time. So much so that I became a seminar leader, traveling the world teaching these life-changing therapeutic techniques and communication tools. Both sciences were highly effective for assisting people to make rapid and lasting behavioral change.

However, I soon realized that getting rid of, or changing, the behaviors I no longer wished to experience in my life was only part of the success puzzle. I needed to get clear about what I wanted to create instead, how I was going to create it, and I needed to do it quickly. I didn't want to take another ten years to make my life the way I wanted it. I was determined to make it happen immediately. This is when I created the Speed Modeling™ method as presented in *Three Steps to Wealth and Power*. Using this method I began to actively research great leaders, thinkers, and achievers to find an alternative route I felt inspired by. As I did this, I also rapidly modeled their attitudes, mindsets, behaviors, and strategies in order to replicate their brilliance in my own life.

Sir Isaac Newton once said, "The reason I see so far is because I stand on the tall shoulders of those who came before me."

I have certainly stood on the tall shoulders of those that have come before me in the creation of this book. Many of the diverse ideas and concepts in *Three Steps to Wealth and Power* will be joined together and presented for the first time. Often, groundbreaking discoveries are the result of bringing together ideas that previously seemed unrelated. For example, Newton's Law of Universal Gravitation was theorized by relating, for the first time, the gravitational pull of planets to objects on Earth. Some of the concepts in *Three Steps to Wealth and Power* have been adapted from the multitude of teachers on my journey, and many of the tools are of my own making. I have put all of these strategies and techniques, as well as my Speed Modeling™ method and the powerful strategies I've gleaned from its use, under the umbrella I call Creation Technologies™.

Creation Technologies™ are the specific techniques that have allowed me to live my grandest ambitions and boldest

9

dreams. I guarantee that should you choose to apply them, they can do the same for you by assisting you to rapidly close the gap between where you are and where you want to be. The "Game of Life" is a powerful analogy to explain the complexities of Creation Technologies™ in a way that is easy to understand. Consequently, I will expand upon this concept throughout this book. Each of us plays a different Game on a different Playing Field with different teammates and all of those factors govern the final result.

We have long since accepted the connection between the mind's thought patterns and success. Many books have even been written on the subject. Perhaps the most famous of these is *Think and Grow Rich* by Napoleon Hill, written in 1960. Still considered a classic self-improvement text to this day, Hill dedicated his life to studying and learning from successful people. *Think and Grow Rich* spawned a tidal wave of similar books over the years, many of them excellent. Yet, typically, I meet thousands of people through my work that, despite reading these books, could not apply the information to their own lives.

Why not?

I believe it is because "success" doesn't mean the same thing to everybody. Therefore, what one success book determines as being successful may not be success for *you*. Each of us is playing a different Game. So how can there be a "one size fits all" approach to success? It is not possible because not everyone is in the same place to begin with. If you wanted to go to Los Angeles, for example, the directions to get you there are very different depending on your current location. How you get to L.A. will depend on whether you are currently in Washington D.C. or in Scotland or Australia.

What *is* possible is to describe the governing principles of success, wealth, and power. For me success is being in a position where I can positively impact people's lives. *Wealth* is living a life of abundance in every area from financial resources to happiness and purpose. *Power* is the ability to effectively produce results in whatever area I choose. For you it may be different but there are certain governing principles that form the building blocks of creation—whatever that creation is for you. These governing principles are: 1) ways of looking at the world and 2) specific techniques that will assist you in navigating yourself from wherever you are right now to exactly where you want to be in your life. Armed with new information and insights, you will plot your own course instead of being at the effect of everything and everyone else.

Oliver Wendell Holmes once said, "A mind that is stretched to a new idea never returns to its original dimension." Some of the ideas presented here may seem alien to you at first; some may be familiar. Some may, as Holmes suggests, stretch your mind so it will never return to its original dimension. Just keep in mind that even if a belief cannot be proven true or false, it can be proven effective or ineffective. In other words, if your particular view of the world is not empowering, you can choose one that is. That is the basis and purpose of Creation Technologies™.

The first step is to wake up to where you are now and get clear on where you want to go. Then find the people who have gone there before you or are heading in that direction and follow their lead. Success is playing the "Game of Life" on your own terms. This, I believe, ultimately comes down to listening to your heart's desire. This book is the modern day version of *Think and Grow Rich* plus the powerful, innovative techniques of today. By using them you can plot your course, and arrive at your chosen destination quicker than you ever thought possible.

STRATEGIC PARTNERING™

The final section of the book is dedicated to techniques and strategies for navigating your way to success. Mastering the art of communication and learning how to inspire others to assist you on your path is essential. Like any team sport, your Game cannot be played and won alone. You cannot win a game of soccer with just a goalkeeper. You need to engage the whole team in a powerful symbiosis. You must learn to harness the power of your teammates to create win-win solutions for everyone. If everyone is inspired by the shared vision and the objective is fulfilling for all, then the whole team marches confidently in the direction of their dreams.

Multi-billionaire Richard Branson did not create his Virgin empire alone. He created it with and through other people. Walt Disney once said, "You can dream up the most beautiful place on Earth, but it takes people to build it." The ability to create strategic partnerships and synergistic relationships is essential to your success. Those who produce extraordinary results are those who can get groups of people working together toward a noble objective.

I'm thrilled to have the opportunity to share this knowledge with you and I hope to meet you at some point in the future on your journey to living the life you deserve!

Step One
WAKE UP!

ONE

Wake Up to Possibility!

"We are boxed in by the boundary conditions of our thinking."
~ Albert Einstein

THE NEW WORLD

Before it was proven that the world was round, it was a well-known "fact" that it was flat. This "fact" was so widely accepted that no one dared dispute it because they thought if they did sail out beyond the horizon they would fall off the edge. In other words, because they believed it couldn't be done, it wasn't done.

That is until Christopher Columbus questioned "common knowledge" and asked "what if?" That question literally expanded the boundaries of his country, changed history and permanently altered accepted reality forever.

In spite of our tendency to think of reality as the non-negotiable basis of our experience, "reality" changes every time someone pushes the boundary conditions of conventional wisdom. When our perception of reality changes, our behavior changes accordingly, based on what is newly considered possible. When Columbus returned from the New World, a revised world map was drawn up and this began a new era of exploration and adventure. Of course, this had always been possible but until Columbus proved it by actually sailing over the horizon and managing to return, people's thinking limited how far they dared to venture and what they dared to attempt.

Examples of the "impossible" being made possible can be found throughout history. When Chuck Yeager flew the X-1, he

15

shattered the myth that there was such a thing as a "sound-barrier." His training and instincts combined with the new technology of the day not only enabled him to go beyond the speed of sound, but reinforced that even alleged technological barriers can be overcome. And what about Roger Bannister? On May 6, 1954, he became the fastest man on the planet when he ran a mile in 3 minutes, 59.4 seconds. The closest anyone had come prior to this was 4 minutes 01.4 seconds in 1945. By breaking the 4-minute mile, a feat previously thought to be humanly impossible, Bannister broke through what Einstein referred to as "the boundary conditions of our thinking." Bannister said at the time, "Now that I have broken the four-minute mile it will be done again—it is like breaking the sound barrier of sport." And he was right—as soon as it was proven possible, many others followed suit and the time was soon beaten.

The self-development tools within this book allow you to breakthrough your own boundary conditions of what you believe is possible in your life, then duplicate the success of others you choose to model and improve upon their success to make it your own.

People often approach me in my seminars with statements such as, "I can't make money. I never had it growing up." Or, "I'll never be successful because my parents never supported me." "I don't have the right education to create wealth," or "I can't pursue my dreams because I have too many obligations." I even hear, "I can't do what I want in my life because I don't have the money." Each one of these individuals is living an illusion. These statements are clear indicators of the boundary conditions of their own thinking. They are accepting certain "truths" about themselves that are then shown to be true by their experience. They are coming up against their own individual horizons beyond which they cannot conceive venturing. They are sure that they are doing battle with external obstacles over which they

THREE STEPS TO WEALTH and POWER *Unleash Your Potential for Unlimited Achievement*

have little or no control. What many people do not yet realize is that these obstacles are just part of the illusion they are creating internally. They have the power to prove *anything* true that they believe and perceive, including more positive outcomes. Success follows belief such as, "I have all I need to be incredibly wealthy and massively successful." Warren Buffett, the most successful investor of all time, was once asked, "How have things changed for you now that you have incredible wealth?" He responded, "Well, I can afford anything I want..." then he paused before adding, "...but then again, I always could."

Even before Buffett had actually created the wealth he had the mindset of wealth, and therefore already had the power to create it because he saw the world in those terms.

"The reasonable man adapts himself to the world," wrote George Bernard Shaw, "the unreasonable one persists in trying to adapt the world to himself. Therefore all progress depends on the unreasonable man." When we dare to go beyond our own internal boundary conditions, we discover a whole new world of possible futures for ourselves.

Let's play a little Game...

It's called the "what's possible" Game. The dictionary definition of possible is "that can, may, be, exist, happen or be done." So for the following questions I want you to answer yes or no. Has someone, somewhere on the planet today, achieved these things?

- Is it possible to have a million dollars in the bank?
- Is it possible to have a successful business?
- Is it possible to wake up excited about life?
- Is it possible to have happy loving relationships?
- Is it possible to be fit and healthy?
- Is it possible to find your life's work and feel passionate about your life most of the time?
- Is it possible to jump off a tall building and fly?

17

Apart from the last question, and please don't test the theory, all of the above are "possible."

Do you agree?

You will no doubt have experienced one of the side effects of this Game as you answered the questions. They are called the "yes, buts." The "yes, buts" are responses such as "yes, but that won't happen to me," or "yes, but that's because they had privileges I don't have," etc. These pesky little side effects come from the little voice in your head. If you're wondering what the little voice is, it's the voice that just said, "what little voice?"

Ignore the "yes, buts" for the time being. All I want you to do right now is open your mind to the possibility that the world is made up of a countless array of experiences from the very worst to the very best. I want you to get your head around the idea and feel comfortable that everything is possible. You may not agree with this at the moment but over the next few chapters I will attempt to prove this to you. I say, "attempt to" because at the end of the day, whether you decide to believe it or not is out of my control. All I can do is present the evidence and ask you to draw your own conclusions. For now I ask that you just allow the idea that all things are possible to exist in your mind.

As someone once said, "a mind is like a parachute—it works best when open." This book is an exploration of the mind. What better way to begin than by prying it open? And here is my promise: if you open your mind as you read this book from start to finish and implement the techniques, you will enjoy a more abundant and fulfilling life. If you find it doesn't serve you, you can slam it shut again—the book and your mind.

TWO

The Playing Field of Life

"For things to change, we must change."
- Henry David Thoreau

So if all things are possible, what is it that dictates what is possible *for you*? Logic would say that the only difference between what is possible and what you experience is *you*.

This diagram illustrates this point:

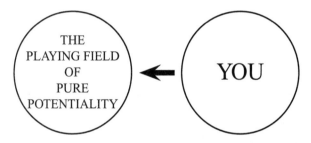

On the left you have the Playing Field of Pure Potentiality. This sphere represents the infinite possibilities in the world—wealth, poverty, great relationships, optimum physical health, disease, depression, happiness, basically everything—everything that is possible, everything that anyone at some point in history has experienced, or someone in the future will experience.

On the right is "You." This sphere represents what you experience in your world. You are the creator of your own world. You are the one who decides what and who becomes a part of it. How much you experience and what you experience is determined only by the extent that you allow yourself to expand and "move into life" by encompassing more of the Playing Field of Pure Potentiality.

The overlap where "You" meet infinite possibility is your unique Game—this represents your current experiences. What Game are you experiencing? Are you happy? Do you experience abundance and power or poverty? Do you feel like a "winner" or "loser?" Are you experiencing fulfilling relationships? Do you want to be?

Over the course of the book, I will explain why it is that you experience what you experience. Remember Einstein's quote at the start of the book, "We are boxed in by the boundary conditions of our thinking." Basically, the size, shape and color of our experience is limited only by the boundaries we put on our thinking over which we don't let ourselves cross.

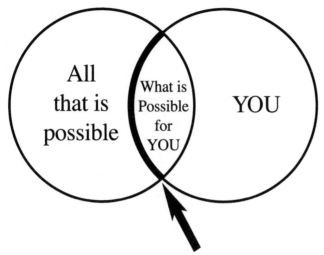

Boundary Conditions of YOUR Thinking

An invisible brick wall limits what we experience. You've probably heard the expression "hitting your head against a brick wall"—this is the brick wall! You may have experienced doing something and then standing back from your action and wondering, "why did I do that?" Or you may have repeated a bad choice over and over again and been perplexed at why. Most of us have experienced that confusion or frustration as to why we continue to do the things we do even when sometimes we know they are not good for us. These are the invisible boundaries at work. The good news is that there are tools to demolish them so that you can make different choices and experience more of what you want and less or none of what you don't want.

Without those tools, our experience of life—the Game we play, can be rather small. And so the Playing Field may look more like this...

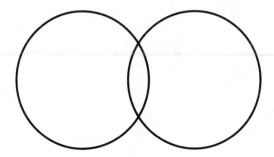

With the tools and knowledge presented in this book, you can expand your experience of life so that the Game you are playing will look like this:

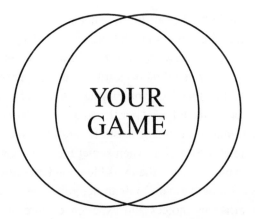

Just think about it for a second. We each live in our own world. Take for example the contrasting worlds of a bodybuilder, a businessman, and a Fijian fisherman.

The professional bodybuilder wakes up early in the morning and heads to the gym. He spends his day planning meals and working his muscles to exhaustion. His life is centered on the upcoming competition for which he has been training zealously over the past several months.

What about the world of a business tycoon? His life is all about the latest deal. He is riding in the back of his limousine reading over the financial statement of a new business in which he is considering investing. He is being driven to the airport where he will board his private jet in order to head out to an important meeting concerning the merger of his company; the merger will soon be made public.

Or the Fijian Fisherman—he wakes up early in the morning and casts his nets out into the ocean. His days are spent catching and cleaning fish and then taking them to the market to sell. In the evening he relaxes sitting on the dock drinking a cold beer and watching the sunset.

Very different Playing Fields—very different Games

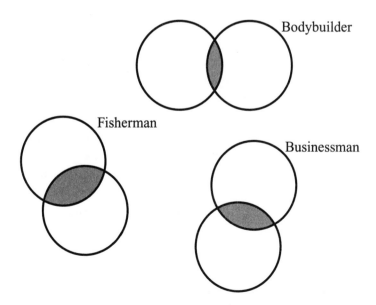

In each case the only difference between their experiences is their choices. Their external world is nothing but a reflection of their internal values, beliefs, attitudes, and the other major filters to their experience. These come together to form the boundary conditions of their thinking, which in turn, creates a different reality for each one.

There is nothing to stop the fisherman from deciding to learn about the stock market and trading online from his oceanside cabin. There is nothing to stop the businessman from hiring a personal trainer and dedicating himself to working out. There is nothing to stop the body builder from giving it all up and becoming a fisherman on a tropical island—nothing that is except the boundary conditions of their thinking.

If you don't already have all the things you wish to be, do or have, you can learn to reprogram your subconscious mind to work in total congruence with your conscious mind to create it all. That is the "Game of Life." Most of us are walking around in a trance of disempowerment, so wrapped up in our worries, fears and doubts that we miss most of the beauty and potential around us. It's time to wake up and learn to use all the creative power you have at your fingertips.

You wouldn't have bought this book if you didn't know that you have more potential than you currently exhibit. Perhaps you find yourself in a position that doesn't fulfill much or any of your highest desires. Perhaps you are playing too small. Once you fully wake up from the "You" as you define yourself, you will be able to fully engage in your "Game of Life" and go for it. Or you may choose a new one to encompass more of the dreams that lie beyond what you currently think is possible.

Take Oprah Winfrey for example. If she had not expanded her view of the world as a child by reading books she would never have risen from the poverty and hardship of her early life to where she is now. Oprah Winfrey is a master of constantly expanding her Playing Field and taking others with her. The way she started was by seeking out possibilities. As she says it, "When I was a young girl growing up in Mississippi I would have never known that anything existed other than the poverty I lived in if it wasn't for the books I read." Reading all those books expanded her references, her self-concept, and therefore, her Playing Field of Potentiality. By doing this she transformed her own reality to play a much bigger Game on a global scale and influenced us all along the way.

You may think you are limited. You are not limited. You can literally expand your potential, your skills, and your abilities at any time as you expand your perceptions of what is possible. Whatever business or relationship you are in, your personal power expands and contracts according to your thinking. Anything you desire that currently seems to you beyond your reach or outside your realm of possibility is only so because it lies just outside the boundary conditions of your thinking in this moment. Your thinking, and therefore what you can achieve, can change in an instant. When Bill Gates was growing up, he read every book on Napolean Bonapart he could find. This stimulated his imagination, expanded what he felt was possible, and thereby changed the world.

Perhaps you are not making the kind of money you feel you deserve and would like to learn to be truly wealthy. Perhaps you feel you are all alone and would like to include phenomenal relationships in your experience. One of the best ways to alter the Game you're playing is to understand yourself better. Seek self-knowledge, combine that with expanding your references by modeling excellence from people that have already achieved the type of success you admire, then apply their strategies to your own life and you will exponentially speed up your journey from where you are now to where you want to be. (I'll explain how to do this in Chapters 4 to 7.) By increasing your understanding and awareness of both yourself and the possibilities that exist in the Universe right now, you are also influencing the scope of your Game.

The size of the Game you choose to play is as much up to you as is the Game itself. You may choose whatever you want and one is no better than the other. The size of the Game is dependent only on the amount of knowledge you are willing to gain. You can be, do, have and create anything you want in life. By increasing your knowledge and understanding of yourself and the true nature of the world and what power is, you automatically increase the size of the Game. That is to say, you increase the Playing Field that you can play upon. That means greater opportunity to create what you want.

THREE

Focus

"You think me a child of circumstances.
I make my circumstances."

~ Ralph Waldo Emerson

Have you ever wondered what separates highly successful people from the rest of the pack? Take multi-billionaire Richard Branson, CEO of the Virgin group of companies, for example. Have you ever wondered what makes Richard Branson, Richard Branson? Here's a guy who has produced massive results in terms of net worth and he seems to attract teams of people who love working for him. Ever wondered what sets someone like that apart? Or what creates a humanitarian such as Gandhi who transformed the face of a nation? Ever wondered what it was that made him take a stand and create change in the country when no one else would? What was it that made him special? Clearly he didn't do that alone. He could not have done it alone. Instead, he mobilized a country to make change without violence by inspiring others with his vision of how the world could be different. What was it that made him step up as the leader to accomplish those things? Or look at Oprah Winfrey. Have you ever wondered what makes Oprah Winfrey, Oprah Winfrey? She was able to create the number one talk show in television history and became a billionaire with an international media empire from a background of poverty. How is that possible?

What makes these people different? What separates them from the rest of the crowd? Those questions are what drove me

27

to develop Creation Technologies™. I had been to all the seminars, read the books, and there were still many facets of my life that weren't working and it was really frustrating. I had seen others who had done the seminars too and although their thinking had shifted on certain levels and things were better in some ways, they still were not able to translate that information and make things happen on a level that I knew they were capable of and I knew I was capable of.

So I started to pour myself into biography after biography in an attempt to find out what was unique about our leaders. We can research movements, thoughts, and ideas until the end of our days, but the true answers to how to create wealth and power lie in the very people who created it themselves. The key lies within those individuals who possessed whatever special combination of traits, thoughts, values, and behaviors it takes to inspire a humanitarian uprising, head a corporate empire or lead a nation.

So I studied those people who moved the world in magical ways and I asked what it was that made the difference. Creation Technologies™ are the result of those years of research.

And this book is the compilation of all the best techniques and ideas that I have found. The more I researched, the more I realized that there were some fundamental characteristics, attitudes, tools, and strategies that made these people stand out. And the really exciting thing about this discovery was that there were common characteristics and all of them are duplicable. Sometimes when we look at those we admire we place them on an untouchable pedestal and assume they are so far away from who we are that their achievements would be impossible to reach. But what I found is that this is simply not true.

There are steps to greatness. Richard Branson didn't suddenly wake up one day a multi-billionaire. Oprah Winfrey didn't suddenly realize she was one of the most influential people in

America overnight. There is a path, a process, and some foundational characteristics that are prevalent in brilliance. Learn those and you can replicate any type of success you choose. First, however you must "clear space" for the new behaviors by discovering what makes *you* tick, what beliefs and attitudes could be coloring your life, so you can ascertain exactly what Game you are currently playing.

FOCUS!

There are two forces at work that govern what you experience. They are inextricably linked and this chapter is dedicated to the first of those—focus. Your world takes on the form that you recognize only once it has passed through your perceptual filters. It's very important to realize that it's completely dependent on the individual as to what information is processed and what information is missed. For example, isn't it possible that the business tycoon may never notice the billboard for the men's bodybuilding competition? Wouldn't you admit that the Fijian fisherman might totally miss the announcement in the financial pages of the business merger? And the professional bodybuilder is less likely than the fisherman to get excited about today's tides. It's not important to them, and therefore, may never appear in their reality.

The *only* thing that determines your concept of reality, the *only* thing that differs between you and someone you admire is what you choose to concentrate your focus on. Your focus creates what is real for you in your world. By changing your focus, I will show you how you can actually change your experiences.

WHAT YOU FOCUS ON DETERMINES YOUR REALITY

In the book *Chaos*, author James Gleick says that the human nervous system is designed to impose order on a chaotic

Universe. All around you is a "quantum soup" of atoms and molecules that are constantly shifting and changing. You create your reality by tuning into and translating certain frequencies that take shape through your perceptions and create what you know as "reality."

Whether consciously or not, in a quantum Universe you choose what to look for and what you experience. In the book *Man's Search for Meaning*, Viktor Frankl describes his experience as a prisoner in four different Nazi death camps in Germany during World War II. Most of his immediate family died in the camps, including his parents, his brother, and his wife. Dr. Frankl, a neurologist and psychiatrist, examines in his book the difference between those who pushed on to survive, and those who gave in to circumstance and withered away, or died in defeat.

The major difference he said was that those who lived focused on a different outcome. They found a way to ascribe a grander purpose or meaning to their current circumstances and existence. By doing this, these people, who were under the most unimaginable conditions, found that there was a larger vision and they saw their current circumstances as being just the thing that would allow them to accomplish that larger vision. Perhaps the very fact that they were there, would be the experience that allowed them to teach the world about the horrors of the holocaust and would be the catalyst to end such terrible atrocities in the world forever. It was this different focus and larger vision that literally kept them alive. And the amazing thing is, whether that belief was true or not, is irrelevant. Having it was what made the difference. By believing something good would come from their experience they were able to survive. So, whether something good did actually come from their experience was not important in the end—they survived! Your focus creates what is real for you in your world. By changing your focus you can actually change your experiences. As was proved by Dr. Frankl and many others, focus can save your life.

You can have whatever you want in life to the extent that you are willing to pay... and what you have to pay is attention.

I am going to explore this concept more fully, including from a quantum physics perspective, but before I do, I want you to really get the concept that your reality is dependent on your focus. One of the best and most powerful ways to do that is through experience. What I want you to do is very simple and will take two minutes. Read how to do the exercise before you do it, so you know what to do:

Have a look around the room or area that you are in right now. I want you to make note of as many things as possible that are blue. Don't write them down. Just take a few moments to notice all the things around you that are blue.

When you are satisfied that you have found as many things as possible I want you to close your eyes and count out on your fingers all of the different objects or things that you remember being blue. No peeking!

Once you have finished, make a mental note of how many things you came up with.

Ready... Go!

Open your eyes. Now flick forward to the end of this chapter and read the question at the bottom of page 38. After you've read the question, close your eyes immediately again—**DO NOT** LOOK AROUND. And answer the question at the end of this chapter. You will count how many things you can remember and make another mental note of that figure. Okay, Go!

Obviously this is slightly more difficult to do in a book than in a live presentation because even if you didn't peek your peripheral vision may have caught a few objects, once the question was raised in your mind. However my guess is that you will have found significantly more blue objects than objects that fit the description of the question at the end of this chapter. I am being deliberately evasive about the question so that this will not make sense unless you do this exercise because I want you to do it. I want you to experience the difference.

So the question is why did you find more blue objects? The answer is simple—you were looking for blue objects. Your focus was to find blue objects and that's exactly what you did.

The same happens in life. So the important question to consider now is, what is it that you are looking for in the world? By working that out you can begin to focus on other things and have other experiences.

This is such a powerful concept on its own it can have a massive impact in your life. It certainly did for a woman who attended one of my trainings. She approached me and mentioned that she was having severe financial problems, yet she desperately wanted to realize her dream of starting a business to help troubled teenagers. I explained to her that there are 13 trillion dollars circulating the planet each and every day and that this is a totally abundant Universe. There are people out there who are literally giving money away, money that she could use to get her business started. She called me two weeks later and said that she had found tens of thousands of dollars available in grant money to launch her new company. The money was always there, she simply had to change her focus in order to pull it into her experience and by doing so she instantaneously changed her world.

This woman had a set view of what was possible in her head and those boundary conditions limited her from expanding her field of vision to see what else was "out there." Changing her focus changed everything.

THE MAP IS NOT THE TERRITORY

In 1933, in the book *Science and Sanity*, linguist Alfred

Korzybski said, "the map is not the territory." What he meant is that your internal representations, thoughts, or internal "maps" are not reality itself. Think about it—the best map of California can never *be* California. Even if it were built to scale and perfectly designed, it still wouldn't be California. Much in the same way, the thoughts that you have about what is happening outside of you can never *be* what is really outside of you.

Your "map" is only a representation of the external circumstances. For example in the movie, "The Great Outdoors," John Candy and Dan Akroyd are looking out at a forest landscape. While Candy's character says, "I look out and I see a beautiful forest with rich natural resources," Akroyd replies, "I look out and I see construction, buildings, and free enterprise." They are both looking at the same thing, but what they see is very different based on their individual models of the world. When Donald Trump passes by a building in New York, he sees something entirely different than the person selling coffee on the street corner.

Most of us think that our perceptions of reality are "the truth," but truth is subjective. For example, say a desperate mother stole some bread from the local shop. Her truth about the event may be that she did what she needed to do to feed her children. The shopkeeper's truth may be she is a thief and should be punished. Is either interpretation wrong or false? Is the mother lying? Is the shopkeeper lying? No. Each is just expressing a different reality based on his or her internal map of the world.

What this means is that there is no such thing as concrete reality. Reality as we think of it is actually a very subjective experience based on each individual. Reality is subject to the expectations of the individual. That means that we do not adapt to reality, as is so often our experience, when we feel we just have to cope with circumstances as they are. Reality adapts to our expectations. We experience what we expect to experience.

This can be such a mind bender for people that it may take a while to wrap your head around it. But don't just take my word for it. This is science—quantum physics. I am fascinated with quantum physics but I also appreciate that it is a complex subject so I will only briefly introduce the evidence regarding the nature of reality. For those curious souls who love to know all the details, I have fully explained the chain of events in quantum understanding in the Appendix at the back of the book. For everyone else, here's a snapshot of what happened.

In the 1950's, in the University of London, physicist, David Bohm suggested that objective "reality" does not exist and that despite an apparent solidity the Universe is essentially an illusion, a gigantic, intricately detailed and complex holographic illusion. Holograms are fascinating because each "part" of the image of a hologram contains the entire image therefore "the whole is in every part."

To simplify it, scientists had decided that the Universe was made up of particles. Previous arguments at the time centered on how those particles communicated with each other. What Bohm said however, was that the particles are not necessarily communicating but rather their separateness is just an illusion. They are part of the whole and the whole is in the part. Bohm argued that at some deeper level of reality such particles are not individual entities, but are actually extensions of the same fundamental whole, whatever that is. This meant at some level that we do not yet understand we are all interconnected. We are all just swimming in a quantum ocean of pure possibility.

Modern science is now restating what the ancient traditions have always held to be true, that you are one with everything in the Universe. Everything is one energy manifesting in almost infinite diversity. As science began to study more and more minute levels of matter they began to see that at the smallest levels, smaller than the atom, there is more space than there is solidity.

In fact, if you examined this book under a high-powered microscope you would see more space than you would solid matter. According to quantum field theorists, the atoms of which the book is made are 99.999 percent composed of the void and emptiness of space. The subatomic particles are impulses of energy and information. What gives the appearance of matter is the arrangement and quantity of the subatomic particles. The density of the arrangement and the vibratory rate determine the form that something takes in the material world.

So a BMW, a pitbull terrier, you, the Grand Canyon, Niagara Falls, The Sydney Opera House, everything in the world right now, is made up of exactly the same "stuff." Look around you right now. Everything that you can see and touch is the same, every person, every object, and every star in the sky. The only thing that is different about each thing is the density and vibrational frequency of the "stuff."

Just as a hologram functions as a sort of lens, a translating device able to convert an apparently meaningless blur of frequencies into a coherent image, the brain also comprises a lens and uses holographic principles to convert the frequencies it receives through the senses into "hard" reality.

If the concreteness of the world is but a secondary reality and what is "there" is actually a holographic blur of frequencies, and if the brain is also a hologram and only selects some of the frequencies out of this blur and transforms them into sensory perceptions, what becomes of objective reality?

Put quite simply, it ceases to exist. As the religions of the East have long upheld, the material world is *Maya*, an illusion, and although we may think we are physical beings moving through a physical world, this too is an illusion.

We are really "receivers" floating through a kaleidoscopic sea of frequency, and what we extract from this sea and interpret into physical reality is but one view taken from an infinite sea of possibility.

Just think about it for a second. If "reality" is different for everyone because everyone translates frequency differently, and therefore, everyone chooses a different experience from a sea of possibility (like the business man, fisherman, and body builder), doesn't it then follow that if you can understand more about the way you translate the frequency, you then have the power to change your world? So if you don't particularly enjoy your current reality you have the opportunity to pluck an alternative reality from the sea of possibility. This book will show you how. In the next two chapters we will unpack all the ways you translate the frequencies to create your current life. With that awareness you can choose whatever experience of life you desire.

As I mentioned earlier, a fuller explanation of the threads of thought that bring us to this conclusion are in the Appendix and for now I trust you can grasp the deep significance of this discovery. There is no reality other than what you choose to create. On some level you are actually experiencing exactly what you "asked" the Universe to deliver. When you choose to focus on the things you want instead of the things you don't want, you begin to play life at a whole new level, a level that works for you instead of against you.

OUR INDIVIDUAL EXPERIENCE OF THE WORLD

Your brain works very much like the worldwide Web. When you go to Yahoo and search for a specific word or phrase, within a matter of seconds you will be presented with all the possible matches for the criteria you entered. All of the millions of other pages of information are left out. You pulled up only what you were looking for. The search engine translated your request and delivered possible solutions to you based on what you asked for.

Your nervous system works the same way. In the book *Flow*,

Hungarian biologist Mihaly Csikszentmihaly says that you are constantly being bombarded by approximately 2,000,000 bits of information per second via the input channels of your five senses. If you were to be instantaneously aware of this external input all at once you would undoubtedly go insane. Your nervous system is designed to cut this massive amount of information down into manageable sizes, or "chunks." Out of 2,000,000 bits of information, you actually process only about 134 bits, or seven chunks (plus or minus two, which means 5-9). So you only process .000067 percent of all of the information coming in. We have this incredible ability to impair our own vision, so to speak, just to keep us from getting utterly overwhelmed. As psychologist Ulric Neisser put it, "our mental machinery knows everything that is going on around us but discards most as unimportant before consciousness is reached."

In the exercise earlier when you were looking for blue objects that's what you found. You punched in "blue" to your search engine and your reality came alive with blue objects. If you did the exercise you will have realized that all the other colors around you melted away as you sought out blue because your focus was blue. So when your focus shifted to the other question you realized you didn't see all of the objects and things that fit that description. Why? Because you were not looking for them. Once again, it's completely dependent on the individual as to what information is processed and what information is not.

Another way to think of it is like this. You live in a dark room. All you've got is one flashlight, which represents your seven plus or minus two chunks of awareness mentioned earlier. Remember, you're being bombarded by 2,000,000 bits of information per second and you're only aware of 134 bits per second. Obviously you're deleting an incredible amount of information! All possibilities exist in this dark room. There is poverty, wealth, poor relationships, great relationships, fitness, vitality, illness, disease, happiness, and depression. What becomes your experience of life is what you choose to shine your light of focus on.

As far back as the 1800's William James, the father of American psychology was quoted as saying, "Focus is everything. If only we had a way to teach it, that would be an education extraordinaire! But it seems to be too difficult to teach."

Well times have changed. I teach thousands of people all over the world in my seminars this "education extraordinaire." Creation Technologies™ is the most powerful approach I have found to take charge of your focus, thereby take charge of your life. The greatest challenge you have at this moment in terms of accomplishing all of your goals is that approximately 90% of the determinants of your focus are still at the subconscious level. All this means is that you may not be aware of what is keeping you from having all that you want. You must first excavate what it is that your subconscious mind is focusing on, so that you can shift that focus to produce better results. And that's what we are going to look at next.

Question: What is yellow?

FOUR

The Rules of the Game

"If a thing is humanly possible,
consider it to be within your reach."
- Marcus Aurelius

Okay, let's just re-group for a second. Suppose that all I have said so far is correct, and I promise you there are far greater minds than mine that have proven it is, what does it mean for you? It means that you have the opportunity to change any and every aspect of your life starting *right now!*

WHAT DETERMINES FOCUS?

I mentioned at the start of the last chapter that there were two factors that governed your experience and they were inextricably linked. The first was focus and the second is your Rule Book, which we will look at now.

Your results in life are dictated by what you focus on. What you focus on is determined by the rules of your Game. You have your own unique rules that govern your life and determine how you view the world—this is your Rule Book. Your Rule Book is largely subconscious and is made up of learned behaviors and personal experiences that have affected your perspective of life. These caused you to draw conclusions about what can and cannot be done, what should and should not be done, and what you can achieve. The tricky part is that most of us don't even know what our own rules are! How can you be expected to win the Game if you don't know the rules?

You created these rules that govern your life. What once was your bible may eventually become your jailer. But just as you wrote it, you can rewrite it to support you in moving towards a future that excites and inspires you.

These rules are what determine what you focus on. Think about it for a moment—if you only process 0.000067% of all the information available to you in any second, who or what decides what you process? That's an incredibly finely tuned search engine, so what are you punching in? If you are experiencing poverty then I hate to have to break this to you, and at some level you are punching in poverty.

The fundamental premise of this book is that nothing is outside of you, and therefore your external world is nothing more than a manifested reflection of your internal world. Yet in order to benefit from that awareness, you must learn to use what is being presented to you in your outside world as a guide to your own internal thinking. That is the paradox.

F. Scott Fitzgerald once said, "The true mark of intelligence is the ability to hold two apparently opposing ideas in the mind simultaneously." Throughout this book you will be challenged many times as we unravel parts of the paradox. The "Game of Life" diagram and analogy gives you a framework and a new perspective to understand that your current "reality" is nothing more than a symptom of your thinking.

One of the things this book will allow you to do is to identify the symptoms and give you the knowledge and practical tools to treat the cause—once and for all. From there you can move into whatever future you desire. It's going to be an exciting and often surprising adventure, and if you play at 100% it will change your life.

The first step is to unravel all the complex components that come together to create this all-important Rule Book. It is this that defines your focus and, therefore, your experience. The good news is, because you created your own rules in the first place, once you know what to look for you can easily access them and recreate them to support you, rather than sabotage you.

So are you ready to understand yourself like you never have before? The rest of this chapter is devoted to uncovering all of the components that operate your life as you know it now. How the mind and body work to create your behaviors is awesome and complex, so be prepared to soak in some fascinating information and just know that once you have gotten through it, you will be that much closer to taking charge of the Game you are playing, then propelling yourself toward ultimate success.

If you really believed that by mastering this information, it would change your life forever, how committed would you be? If you knew that by following through on the exercises in this book you could have all you desire, how much of yourself would you pour into learning the information? My guess is that you would be *very* committed. Do yourself a favor and be willing to accept the possibility that you truly could have the life you envision for yourself and commit to this transformation now.

Here we go...

DETERMINANTS OF FOCUS:
YOUR RETICULAR ACTIVATING SYSTEM

Located at the base of the brain, the Reticular Activating System (RAS) is responsible for a number of functions but the one we are interested in is called filtering. This is the process that determines what you become conscious of and what remains in the forefront of your mind, and what simply disappears into the recesses of your subconscious. The RAS is like your own in-built newspaper editor. It decides what is put on the front page and what is to be put on page thirty or relegated to archive before it even hits the press!

Whether you are conscious of it or not, you tell the RAS

what to look for. This is one of the reasons why it's important to write down goals. This action activates the RAS and tells your brain to look out for opportunities or information that will allow whatever it is you want to become a reality. In addition to the biological filters of the RAS, which are unique to us as a species, you also have internal filters that cause your subjective reality to take form. The RAS interprets the rules of the "Game of Life."

THE FILTRATION PROCESS

In order to cut down on the overwhelming amount of information coming in through the five senses, your nervous system does the job of deleting, distorting, and generalizing the information.

DELETIONS, DISTORTIONS, AND GENERALIZATIONS

Deletion, distortions and generalizations are the techniques your mind uses to reduce the information registering in the conscious mind to a manageable amount based on your ground rules—what you are "sorting for," or expect to experience. These are the "big picture" techniques that aim to chunk higher, squash together or remove information from your radar screen.

1. Deletion—I am sure you have had the experience where you've gone to buy a new car or a new suit or pair of shoes and the moment you decide on the item, you see it everywhere. Say you decided to buy a red Toyota and red Toyotas started appearing in your reality. It wasn't that red Toyotas suddenly manifested everywhere you looked. They were always there; you just didn't see them until they were important to you. You had simply never noticed them before, because up until that point, you had been deleting them from your experience.

Deleting information is simply the process of leaving out

large amounts of data that your Rule Book has deemed unimportant to your life at that time. An example of a deletion would be the businessmen and the fisherman we talked about earlier. The merger of the businessman's company may reach the business press, but if it is of no consequence to the fisherman it will be deleted from his experience or awareness. If, however, the fisherman got tired of getting up so early and decided he would buy and sell stock and he invested money into the businessman's company, you can guarantee that mention of the merger in the newspaper would then catch his attention because suddenly it IS important to him. So the RAS added it to his awareness.

Your experience of life is largely dependent upon what you are deleting at any given moment. You get what you focus on and you don't experience that which you delete.

2. Distortion—Distortion can often appear as the process of interpreting incoming information as something other than what consensual reality says it is. One form of distortion is seeing, hearing, or feeling something that's not actually there. When you think you hear someone say something that wasn't actually said, that's a distortion.

When Al Gore and George W. Bush were having recounts of the votes that were cast in Florida to decide the 2000 presidential election, the country was sharply divided on how to proceed. The division was largely based on political affiliation. People who supported the Republican Party *distorted* the situation to support their values and beliefs, while people who supported the Democrats *distorted* everything that occurred to support *their* values and beliefs. It is certain that if the situation had been reversed, the Democrats would have won the machine vote. The distortions would have been reversed as well, and they would have simply swapped roles. This is a classic example of distortion!

As with deletion, the ability to distort is a very important function of the human nervous system. If you weren't able to distort information and you met someone for the first time, you would not recognize him or her again were they to change clothes, or change their appearance in some other way. Sometimes your distortions empower you, but sometimes they don't. The Game is all about choosing an internal process that is empowering. By taking more control of this, otherwise subconscious process, we empower ourselves to produce the results that we most desire.

3. Generalization—The third of the three ways you filter information is by generalization. Generalization is a valuable process because it is what allows you to remember and categorize things once you've learned them. When you were a child you learned that a certain object was called a chair and is used to sit on. You were then able to generalize that similar objects were also called chairs and were also used to sit on. Without the ability to generalize, you would have to relearn what the object is and the purpose it serves each time you see a different *type* of chair. Your generalizations, like the other filtration processes, can serve you well, but they can also limit you in your life.

Generalizations make up your belief systems, or the specific rules you have that govern your life. If you have a generalization or a belief that "chairs are used to sit on," you will sit on them when you need to. Just as an example, imagine if you had a bad experience with a chair when you were younger. What would happen if say, you sat on a chair that was missing a leg, and you fell down and hurt yourself? As a result, your subconscious mind, in order to protect you in the future, might generalize that all chairs are bad. In a case like that, the process of generalization would actually hinder you, because it might take away choices in the future that involved sitting on chairs.

Many people generalize in ways that eliminate choices for them in life. They form beliefs or rules such as "money and happiness don't go hand in hand," or "I could NEVER be successful," or "You can't make money without cheating people," or "I could never make a positive global impact." This is when the generalizing function is used in a disempowering way.

What you delete, distort, and generalize is dependent on your internal filters. These filters are your Rule Book and are created through your upbringing, your environment, and the significant emotional experiences in your life. They determine what you focus on, look for, or "sort for," and what is left out of your experience of reality. These filters are comprised of values, beliefs, attitudes, memories, decisions, language, and Meta Programs. As John McCrone writes in *How the Brain Works*, "A person is a collection of memories and habits that shapes the moment to moment flow of the mind."

It is important that you now start to recognize yourself in these categories by beginning the process of self-awareness. As you read through the next section, consider how each filter applies to you specifically. Which rules do you operate with? There are no right or wrong answers, only what is right for you. This not only helps you to understand yourself better but also helps you to recognize certain filters in others, which is extremely useful not only when modeling excellence but in managing and leading people.

After you have read through this section the next chapter is all about digging out your own Rule Book from the recesses of your mind, so you can become very clear as to the rules by which you are currently playing the "Game of Life." Once you have clearly identified where you really are, not where you wish you were, you are truly in a position to make lasting change.

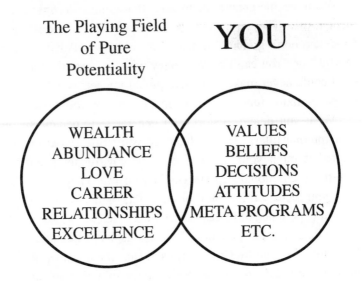

The Playing Field of Pure Potentiality

YOU

WEALTH
ABUNDANCE
LOVE
CAREER
RELATIONSHIPS
EXCELLENCE

VALUES
BELIEFS
DECISIONS
ATTITUDES
META PROGRAMS
ETC.

INTERNAL FILTERS—
YOUR RULE BOOK FOR REALITY

1. Values

The first of the seven filters is Values. Values are those things that you consider important in life. These are some of the major filters that will determine where you spend your time and what Game you play. Values are broad concepts that guide your decisions in life. They are what you stand for and the foundation of your character.

Since everyone's values differ, each of us has a different experience of living. An individual who values wealth will invest time and effort in that area and his or her experience of life will reflect that. If that same person does not value honesty then the route to wealth would be very different than someone who values both wealth and honesty highly.

I had a good friend come to me for coaching because he wasn't producing the results that he wanted in his physical health. He was a financially successful executive who ran three different companies but he was running his physical health into the ground. I proceeded to elicit his life values by asking him the question, "What's important to you in life?" He listed a number of different things including entrepreneurialism and financial success but, interestingly enough, health was not even included on his list. Because your values determine where you spend your time, the root cause of his issue was clearly a values issue. Recognizing this was the first step for him in terms of turning his health around.

2. Beliefs

The second internal filter is your beliefs. Beliefs are your convictions, those things that you consider true in life. If you believe that you can learn anything that you put your mind to regardless of age, your experience of life is going to be very different from that of someone who believes that they are not that smart and couldn't possibly learn something new.

Your beliefs form the parameters of your Game. These make up some of the boundary conditions of our thinking that Einstein referred to. Your beliefs will narrow your possible experiences as fast as any other filter. When transformed, beliefs will also give wings to your potential and allow you to soar to new heights.

There was a talented woman who attended one of my seminars and she told me that she was an artist. She absolutely loved what she did, but she wasn't making the kind of money that she wanted. After doing some exploration it was revealed that she had a belief that women could not make "real money" in art. This belief was preventing her from focusing on all of the money-making opportunities that existed for her. Identifying the limiting belief was the precursor for obliterating it. Soon after that, her income doubled.

3. Attitudes

Attitudes are the third set of filters. Attitudes are abstract ideas that are made up of "clusters" of beliefs and values around a given subject. It is a frame of mind built on your values and beliefs. They are often quite hard to pinpoint because they are less solid and can therefore, be quite insidious. They can distort your perspective positively or negatively. When people talk of "seeing something through rose-colored glasses" they are referring to a person's attitude. For example, the person who has a positive attitude toward work and sees it as a place to self-actualize while creating value for others, will have a very different experience than someone who has a negative attitude toward work and sees it only as a means to pay bills.

A woman came to me once for coaching, stating that she wanted to lose some weight because she said that it would make her feel better about herself, give her more energy, and positively effect the results she was producing in her career. I suggested that in order to make the changes she wanted to make, she would have to change her eating habits. She was, however, adamant she wasn't prepared to do that. She assumed that if she worked with a results coach she would be able to miraculously get results without changing anything! I explained the law of cause and effect where every action creates an equal and opposite reaction. If she didn't change her actions, she couldn't change the result of her actions. She chose not to continue, yet her attitude was the only thing standing between her and the outcome she desired.

4. Memories

Memories also filter your current experience of reality. You evaluate your world through your memories and the experiences that you have. Memories can be the cement or rationale that keeps a belief in place. Yet they are only stored snapshots of a multi-dimensional event that took place. You only have the left-over remnants of whatever segments of that event you processed through your perceptual filters at that time. So for example, an Alsatian dog runs up to you when you where three years old. You are very scared because an Alsatian is a large dog. In that moment you make a neurological connection between dogs and being scared. As an adult you may not even remember the incident of being scared by the dog, and you nonetheless feel scared of dogs. You have used the old memory to ascribe the same or similar meaning, which then directs your emotional reaction in the present. You may not even be aware why anymore.

Even though the memory may be twenty years old or more, it can trigger your interpretation and perception of the current situation based on your subjective experience at the time of the original incident. One particular gentleman in our seminars mentioned that when he was growing up, his parents were constantly arguing about money. Because he had no other references to prove otherwise, he mentally linked the two ideas together and formed the conclusion that money equaled unhappiness. As a result, he made an unconscious choice never to have any money, since "that was what spoiled relationships." With the techniques presented in this book, he was then able to expand his positive references and thus expand his Playing Field and change the Game he was playing to include an abundance of money.

5. Decisions

Decisions are also one of the major filters of your experience. Throughout your life you make decisions both consciously and unconsciously as to the meaning of the things that happen in your subjective reality. If memories are the cement that perpetuates a belief, then decisions are the cornerstones of belief. They act as the line in the sand from which you will make future choices. Every belief is preceded by either a conscious or subconscious decision to accept that belief.

Someone who decides early in life that they will one day become President of the United States of America will have a different experience of life than someone who decides that they will never amount to anything. A woman in one of my seminars had made a decision at an early age that "this is a man's world" and she would have to struggle and work many times harder in order to achieve only moderate success. Therefore, she continually sorted for, or looked for, every example in her experience that would back up the previous decision she had already made subconsciously about life. We tend to get what we look for. Her present life reflected a decision she had made a long time ago. This all changed for her in one of our weekend seminars by using the Creation Technologies™ tools to obliterate the limiting decision.

6. Language

Language is also a powerful filter. Linguist Max Muller states it this way, "We can as little think without words as we can breathe without lungs." The language that you use can actually determine what concepts are available to you, and therefore your experience in life. Analytical philosophers and linguists as varied as Arthur Schopenhauer and Muller have all stressed the point that language is what allows us to take our minds and consciousness to previously unexplored places.

An animal such as a cat or a dog can only think in relation to the present tense. For example, a cat cannot imagine what it might be doing two days from now. It is language that allows human beings to transport themselves mentally to imagined viewpoints or even to consider how we might be perceived from other points of view. Because language determines what we can think about it also determines what we see in the world.

Ludwig Wittgensein once said, "Whereof one cannot speak, one cannot think." I saw an amazing demonstration of this once on a television talk show on which a Native American Indian chief was being interviewed. One of the things that he mentioned was that his particular tribe has no word in their language for "war," therefore, he emphasized, war did not exist for them.

If you want to be rich, one of the things you need to do is to increase your financial vocabulary. The moment you begin to increase your financial vocabulary, you begin to open up the limits you have placed on your experience therefore, you shift your focus and change your Playing Field. How can you think like an investor if you don't know the language of investing? Business and investing have a language of their own. Understanding financial ratios and financial statements requires an awareness of all of the terms associated with them. When you understand the terms, your mind can think in new ways that were previously unavailable.

I had a friend who was taught early in life that one shouldn't speak about financial matters because it was inappropriate and money was not important. His parents told him relationships and love were more important than money. I don't necessarily disagree with that idea but who says you can't have both?

Because he never discussed money he never learned how to think in financial terms and consequently found himself without money.

How do you increase your financial vocabulary? Read new types of materials, have new conversations with people. Warren Buffett, the world's most successful investor was once asked to reveal the secret of his success and he replied, "I read over 2000 annual reports a year."

7. Meta Programs

Meta Programs are the last set of filters that determine your experience of the world. They are context-dependent, content free, filters that determine your experience in life. There are several Meta Programs listed below as well as descriptions of each of the patterns. As you read over these descriptions consider how you filter the world. To assist you to get a better understanding of how you operate, circle the filter that most describes how you function. This will also give you a good understanding of how to recognize these filters in yourself, so you can then start to recognize them in others, which is very important for modeling.

Motivation Filter

Do you move primarily "toward" what you want in life or "away from" what you don't want? If you are propelled toward what you want then positive statements such as "money will give me freedom and a sense of achievement" will motivate you. If you move away from what you don't want, negatively expressed statements such as "money will mean I'll never be broke again" will motivate you.

"Away from" motivation can provide a powerful "push" but it will tend to produce inconsistent results for a couple of different reasons.

If your primary motivation is, "not wanting to be broke" or "having to pay the bills," you are actually focused on "being broke" and "paying the bills." The subconscious mind cannot process a negative statement directly. So in this instance if I say, "I don't want to be broke," the brain must first think about being broke in order to *not* think about being broke. Because we tend to get what we focus on in life, if being "broke" and "paying the bills" is your focus, this will tend to be all that you experience.

Also from a motivation perspective, if you want money because you "don't want to be broke," or "have to pay the bills," this is called pain motivated performance. Pain motivated performance will still push you, but the moment you are no longer broke (if you are lucky enough to make it there) or the moment that you have paid all the bills, your motivation disappears, which will tend to cause cyclical performance.

If you are totally "away from" motivated it's likely that you will have inconsistent performance. If you are on the extreme of "toward" motivation you may never get around to doing those things that are necessary for the maintenance of the result. In order to determine whether you are "toward" or "away from" motivated, think about a short or long term goal then ask yourself the question, "what is important to me about achieving that goal?" Notice if your responses are primarily rooted in what you want or what you don't want.

Then you can determine if you are:
  a) Toward motivated
  b) Toward with a little away
  c) Both toward and away equally
  d) Away with a little toward
  e) Away from motivated

Orientation Filter

This filter is similar to the motivation filter although it has more to do with whether you do what you do in life because of the possibilities you look forward to or out of a sense of necessity or obligation. If you are necessity oriented you will tend to operate based upon what you are "supposed" to do or "should" do, whereas if you are possibility oriented you will tend to act based upon what you "can" do or "could" accomplish. The question you can ask yourself in order to determine whether you are primarily possibility or necessity oriented is "why am I choosing to do what I'm doing in my career?" Notice if your response tends more toward a sense of possibility or necessity or both in equal measure.

Are you:
  a) Possibility
  b) Necessity
  c) Both

Success Indicator Filter

This filter determines how you evaluate your performance. Do you look for external verification on how you are doing or do you just know inside yourself how you've done? Are you more concerned with what others think or with what you think? The question to determine your frame of reference is, "what or who lets me know I've done a good job?" Notice whether your answer is based on internal or external indicators.

Are you:

    a) Internal

    b) External

    c) Internal with external check

    d) External with internal check

Decision-making Filter

This filter determines what internal representation system you use to make a decision. Do you have to *see* evidence that convinces you, do you have to *hear* the evidence, *read* about it, or prove it to yourself by *doing* it? This filter will also tend to determine how you know you've truly learned something. Ask yourself, "What do I need to make my decision about a proposal? Do I have to see it, hear about it, read about it, or do it with them?"

Do you:

    a) See

    b) Hear

    c) Read

    d) Do

Convincer Filter

This filter determines how often you need to go through your decision-making strategy before you are convinced of anything. We all have subconscious strategies for making decisions, which are simply the order and sequence of steps that need to occur in order to make any given decision. The convincer demonstration filter is determined by asking yourself, "How many options do I need to weigh before I can make a choice?" Are you able to make a decision immediately? Do you decide after looking at a couple of options? Do you need a certain period of time before you can make a decision about something, or do you need to be consistently convinced?

Are you:

a) Automatic
b) A number of times
c) A period of time
d) Consistent

Leadership Filter

This filter tells us if you know what you need to do in order to be successful at any given task, if you know what others need to do, and if you find it easy or not so easy to tell them what they should do. If you are "self only" you will be effective at leading your own life although you may not be able to manage others because you don't find it easy to tell them what to do. If you are "self and others" you are able to lead your own life as well as manage and direct others. If you are "self but not others" you know what you need to do in order to be successful but have no idea what other people need to do, therefore you will certainly have difficulty leading other people. Finally if you are "others only" you will have no idea what you need to do to be successful but you know what everyone else needs to do. Ask yourself the question, "What could I do to improve my performance at work?" Then, "What could my coworkers do?" If you find it easier to know what others could improve on than yourself, then ask yourself, "Could I easily tell them what they could improve on?"

Are you:
- a) Self only
- b) Self and others
- c) Self but not others
- d) Others only

Energy Direction Filter

This filter will determine where you direct your energy when pursuing your life goals. You will be either more active or reflective in life. If you are at the far extreme of activity you will take massive action toward your goals, so much so that sometimes you will jump into the pool and then check to see if there is water in it afterwards. If you are more reflective you will tend to do a detailed study of all the consequences of action before taking it. Reflection at its extreme can lead to paralysis of analysis, where no action is taken and you just sit back and let the world pass you by. Ask yourself the question, "When I come into a new situation do I usually take action immediately or do I conduct a detailed study of all of the consequences before acting?"

Are you:
- a) Active
- b) Reflective
- c) Both
- d) Inactive

Performance Filter

This is different from the energy direction filter in that it speaks more of where you gain your greatest pleasure in your career path, and therefore where you perform optimally. Do you prefer situations in which you are a solo or independent player? Do you prefer to be part of a team or do you prefer to lead a team? Ask yourself the question, "What gives me the greatest enjoyment at work? When I am working on my own, as part of a team, or when I am leading a team?"

Are you:
   a) Independent player
   b) Team player
   c) Management player

Work Satisfaction Filter

Do you prefer to work with things, systems, or people? If you like to work with *people* you will often describe the joys of interacting with others when talking about work. If you are more inclined to work with *systems* you will often talk about the systems in place that make work compelling. If you get satisfaction from working with *things* you might talk about the specific things you do when describing your work. Ask yourself the question, "What do I particularly enjoy about what I do for work?"

Do you prefer:
   a) Things
   b) Systems
   c) People

Preferred Interest Filter

The preferred interest filter is similar to the work satisfaction filter, although it relates more to what you focus on in life rather than from a work perspective specifically. Ask yourself, "What do I enjoy spending my time doing?" Do you think more about the people you spend time with, the places you go or live, the things or objects you come in contact with, the activities you take part in, or the information and learning you gather?

Are you:
   a) People
   b) Places
   c) Things
   d) Activity
   e) Information

Abstract/Specific Filter

Are you an abstract thinker or do you operate more on the plane of specificity? If you are abstract you see the big picture. At the extreme of this range you could find the spiritual person who is interested only in the relationship with God, love, or light. At the other end of the spectrum would be the accountant who is only interested in numbers.

The thinking pattern filter holds a direct relationship to the amount of money that you make in life. The global thinker has the "big picture"; this will tend to be the C.E.O., entrepreneur, or visionary. The detailed thinker will tend to be the janitor or errand runner. The trick, however, is to be able to move throughout the range from abstract thinking to specific thinking. There are also abstract thinkers who are not sufficiently "grounded" to produce results in the material world. The magician of the material world is that person who can weave the abstract vision and then reach up into the ethers and pull it down into enough specificity to produce real world results. Ask yourself the question, "What are my future goals?" Then see if you focus on the big picture and abstract feelings or specific numbers of how much you want to be worth and certain things you want to have along the way. Then see if your mind moves from the big picture to the specifics or vice versa.

Are you:
- a) Specific
- b) Abstract
- c) Specific to abstract
- d) Abstract to specific

Comparison Filter

This filter relates to what relationships you tend to see between people and how you compare things. Do you look for the similarities or the differences? The sameness person will tend to like routines. They do not care for change and find security and comfort in sameness. The differences person on the other hand is someone who craves variety and will tend to notice the differences in things. Ask yourself the question, "What's the relationship between these three coins?"

Notice if you focus on the similarities or differences.
Are you:

   a) Sameness

   b) Sameness with exceptions

   c) Sameness with differences equally

   d) Differences with exceptions

   e) Differences

Challenge Response Filter

Are you a feeling person who tends to let their feelings run your life or are you more dissociated and thinking in your approach? Another possibility is that you could be at choice and can operate in either thinking or feeling modes at will. Think of an event in your career that gave you trouble or was challenging to you personally and ask yourself, "did I react in a way that was more feeling, thinking, or did I have a choice between the two?"

   Are you:

   a) Thinking

   b) Feeling

   c) Choice

Time Awareness Filter

Do you plan your life out or live freely in the moment taking each day as it comes? If you are a *through time* person you will tend to be very time conscious. You live life in relation to time and will not tend to be late and you'll have a good idea of your goals or ambitions or the direction you're heading in life. You'll likely have your goals mapped out on a timeline. If you are an *in time* person on the other hand, you will be more interested in living in the moment. You have less direction and care more about fully experiencing the now, which can mean you are often late and have less awareness of time.

Are you:

a) Through time

b) In time

Focus Filter

This final Meta Program relates to whether you are primarily focused on yourself or other people.

A major airline used this filter when they were hiring staff. During the interview process each candidate was asked to stand up in front of the group and give a short presentation on themselves. What the candidates were not aware of was that they were being monitored not based on how well they spoke or presented, but on how well they listened to the other candidates when they spoke. It was a brilliant strategy for hiring natural service-orientated people. Each of the candidates were under pressure to perform and do their best so it tested whether they were more interested in themselves and how well they would do or were they still focused on those around them.

Are you:

a) Self

b) Others

Your values, as well as your beliefs, attitudes, and Meta Programs, are instilled at an early age, based upon those of your parents and whether you accepted or rejected theirs. Many of these filters change as you grow older and continue to be shaped by society, peer influences, and significant emotional events.

This Rule Book of beliefs, values, and other filter patterns that you have created is real, but only to you as an individual.

INTERNAL FILTERS

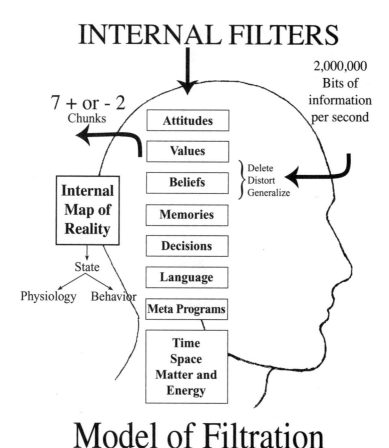

Model of Filtration

Your model of the world is as unique as your thumbprint. All of your internal filters effect your life dramatically. Let's look at beliefs for a moment. One distinction that I have made about beliefs is that it does not matter whether they are true, right or real. What is important is whether or not a belief that you hold produces the results you want in your life. A belief is nothing more then a generalization about the world or your ability that then determines what behaviors and actions you allow yourself to experience. For every idea there is always a counter example that could prove it untrue. What's important to understand about generalizations is that they are all just opinions, including this one. So the question to ask is, are my beliefs creating the behaviors and experiences that I prefer? Most people think that the world they experience is unchangeable. I hope that having read the previous chapter you are starting to see that need not be the case.

Think about it. If somebody said that the reason they were not successful was because they didn't go to college, the presupposed belief or generalization is that people who don't go to college are unsuccessful and that people who do go to college are successful. This generalization has the potential of giving a person a reason or excuse not to explore certain options in life and excel. If a person has that belief they may not go after a high paying job because they believe that those are reserved for people who have gone to college. This type of thinking can limit the results that you produce in life by preventing certain avenues from being explored.

Now, is this belief true? It doesn't matter. What matters are the results that you produce by either having it or not having it. If Bill Gates had the belief that you need a degree to be successful, he might not have dropped out of Harvard to start Microsoft and become the richest man in the world eleven years later. There are many examples of people that have gone to college and become very successful. There are also people that have gone to college and been spectacular "failures." The point is, it doesn't matter. Whether you did or didn't get an education is not what will stop you from achieving your dreams. What can and will stop you are the limiting beliefs that make it okay for you to not even try.

Simply educating yourself and learning new things can have the effect of changing your internal filters. For example, the more I learned about personal finances, the more it became important to me to create wealth in my life. This changed my values considerably. The more I learned about how to produce results in the world, the more I realized the true power that we can all access. At that point, I felt a responsibility to help shape the world in positive ways and make sure that as many people as possible get this information and these skills of empowerment. My new understanding of how manifestation works also changed my values considerably. It is possible to change your filters through education. In some of our live seminar programs, we also teach how to change your major filters instantaneously using powerful techniques for accelerated human change.

It is important to remember that although the process of deletion, distortion, and generalization are your "first cut" techniques for perceiving "reality," they are inextricably linked to the more detailed filters because it is the unique combination of these filters that determines what you will delete, distort, and generalize. This has tremendous significance because when you realize what you consider to be "real" in your experience is nothing but a fraction of what's really out there, you begin to redirect your focus and actually choose what appears in your reality. You then begin to gain control over what you sort for or look for, therefore, what you experience in life. Your experience becomes more positive and in line with what you desire.

FIVE

What Rules Are You Playing By?

"We do not see things as they are; we see things as we are."
~ The Talmud

Before we explore what your particular rules are, I want to explain a couple of really exciting things. The first is a concept called perception is projection.

PERCEPTION IS PROJECTION

Psychologists since Freudian times have spoken of the concept of "projection" and "perception is projection." Essentially what this means is that you can't see anything outside of you that isn't you. So examining an area of your life that you are currently not happy with can hold extraordinary insights about what you believe about life. If, for example, you don't have as much money as you would like, this is a clear indication that at some level you have one or more limiting beliefs about money. You may not be consciously aware of them, but they are there. Once you know they are there, you can set about uncovering them and bringing them into conscious awareness. Simply by doing that, the limiting beliefs lose their power over you. You can then start to create new results in the realm of wealth creation.

I encourage you to see your current life as a reflection of your thinking, a benchmark of your own psychological understanding and strength. Your experience is an accurate and

65

ruthless measure of what you are currently communicating to the Universe about who you are and what you will and will not accept in your life. This is your opportunity to use your circumstances and situations as a way of understanding yourself better. And that is empowering. If you can use your so-called "failings" as a compass toward success you will reach your destination in a fraction of the time. You no longer just hope that you are going in the right direction while running blindly down alley after alley, instead you plot a true course.

The reason this is so important and so powerful is because once you start to unpack your life you can look at different areas and see what is working and what is not. Both hold clues to your ultimate success.

Over the past decade I have taught live seminars around the world. I worked with thousands and thousands of people and one of the things that constantly fascinates me is that people are basically the same no matter color, culture, or creed. One of the most disempowering similarities I have found time and time again is the blanket generalizations that people place over their own lives. By definition, those who are looking for change are usually the same people that wind up in one of my programs. I absolutely applaud each and every one of those people because they have taken a critical first step toward change, as have you in reading this book. What I have noticed however is that we are usually far harder on ourselves than anyone else ever is. So I might talk with someone and ask what his or her life is currently like and often the response is something like, "Oh it's terrible, nothing is working." Yet when I press for specifics they are able to see that it's not actually that *nothing* is working, just certain areas of their life. And there may very well be areas that they are completely overlooking as positive influences in their world. For example, they may be happily married or have a wonderful relationship with their children or be very fit and healthy yet, these areas are ignored as they strive for more money in the bank or the next promotion. So right now I want you to get clear about what areas of your life are working and which ones don't appear to be working at the level you would like. Know that both are very powerful as they each provide sign posts for improvement that I will explain along the way.

Based on my experience, I have categorized the various areas of life that most people are interested in. With each one I want you to be honest and give yourself a score from 1-10, ten being the highest sense of satisfaction and success, one being the lowest. If there are others that spring to mind for you, add them.

_____ Relationship/Love
_____ Family life
_____ Financial
_____ Health and fitness
_____ Contribution in the community
_____ Spiritual growth
_____ Friendships
_____ Career

_____ _____
_____ _____

My hope is that this exercise will give you some perspective about what you want to change, what currently works or doesn't work, what you want to improve and focus on, and what you are content with as it is. This information will help you as you move through the book.

You can now run the following exercise on any one of the categories above or, as will be explained, on your life as a whole. I encourage you to run the exercise on separate categories and compare the highest scoring category with the lowest scoring category. This can be incredibly powerful as it lets you see the beliefs that sit behind your experience. You will no doubt experience the areas of your life that work better are supported by empowering, healthy values, and beliefs. Those areas that don't work are not.

HOW TO DETERMINE YOUR HIDDEN RULE BOOK

Part of getting what you want and getting where you want to go is knowing where you are now. You have already identified your Meta Programs, which is part of your Rule Book. Now it's time to take a closer look at the rest of the components that make up your subjective experience of reality. As you go through the following exercise, be honest with yourself and keep in mind that you will be transforming your Rule Book as you progress through the book.

Life Values: Ask yourself the question, "What's important to me in life?" Your responses should be single words or short phrases. Make a complete list below.

_____

_____

_____

_____

_____

_____

_____

_____

Once you've listed all of your values, or what's important to you, it's time to number them in order of importance. When you do this make sure you order them the way they really are, not the way you wish they were. For example, if you say that wealth is your #1 value but you spend your time playing Nintendo all day, it's most likely that wealth isn't really your #1 value. Maybe freedom, fun, or relaxation is higher than you thought. Because values provide our upfront motivation it's likely that you will either be actualizing your highest values or you'll be spending a good portion of your time on them. Values differ from goals in that goals require steps to achieve them while your values are something you live everyday. So order the values you stated above in order of importance below, according to which are actually showing up in your life the most and least?

1._____

2._____

3._____

4._____

5._____

6._____

7._____

8._____

9._____

10._____

When people list their values in their true order of importance as you have just done above, it can be an eye-opener and even disillusioning. Disillusionment is good. It's the first step to making the changes you desire. Next, you'll take a look at your beliefs. Because beliefs have such a huge effect on what you will ultimately experience in your life, it is important to work out what they are too. What you will find when you think about these questions is that many of your assumptions about life have been handed down to you by your family. Others may have come from your own experience.

This is an illuminating process for most people. Often we are genuinely shocked by some of the things that spring to mind regarding our ability and worthiness to be, do, and have all we desire. These beliefs have been cobbled together and taken as true often without your conscious awareness. You accepted these rules in the first place, so you can also choose to change your mind and install a new Rule Book.

To illustrate this point, I want you to write down three outrageous goals. Three results that you would desire if you had no limits and you could live your wildest dreams. Write down one in the context of your life's path, one in the context of your finances, and one in the context of what you would contribute to the world.

Life's Path

_____

_____

_____

_____

_____

_____

Finances

_____

_____

_____

_____

_____

_____

Contribution to the World

_____

_____

_____

_____

_____

_____

Once you've written down the three goals, the next step is to write down everything that is preventing you from achieving those goals. For example, you might say, "I'm too young," or "I'm too old," "I don't have the education," or "I don't have the resources or contacts I need."

Make a list below of everything that is preventing you from achieving those three goals.

_____

_____

_____

_____

_____

_____

_____

_____

_____

_____

_____

_____

These are the boundary conditions of your thinking or your limiting beliefs. Next, it's time to discover some of your traits and attitudes. List below the traits that you believe those who know you well would describe you as having:

_____

_____

_____

_____

_____

_____

_____

_____

_____

_____

Now list the attitudes that you would describe yourself as having specifically in relationship to your life's path, your career, and your finances. Be honest with yourself.

_____

_____

_____

_____

_____

_____

_____

_____

_____

_____

Congratulations! You are making real progress towards the wealth and power you desire. It's been said that a problem well-stated is a problem half-solved. Understanding your own hidden Rule Book, which has up to this point determined what Game you are playing, empowers you to change your rules, change the terrain, and change the results of your Game!

Step Two

CHOOSE YOUR GAME

So if objective reality does not exist and instead all that exists right now is your personal reality, based on your own Rule Book, much of which is subconscious, then it's time to decide now what Game you would like to play and master the rules! You are ready to harness the power of Speed Modeling™.

SIX

Model the Change You Want to Be

*"Most everything I've done,
I've copied from someone else!"*
~ Sam Walton

As natural as Oprah Winfrey seems at what she does, there was a time that she was completely insecure and had to go through a period of trial and error before she really had a basis from which to launch her own unique style and niche. She has said, "When I did my first audition for my first television job, I was such a nervous wreck, I had no idea what to do or say. I thought in my head that maybe I'll just pretend I'm Barbara Walters. I will sit like Barbara and hold my head like Barbara. So, I crossed my legs at the ankles, I put my little finger under my chin, I leaned across the desk, and I pretended to be Barbara Walters." Modeling is something you have been doing your whole life without being aware of it. The only problem is most of us model haphazardly without conscious awareness. Now, over the course of the following three chapters you will learn how to consciously choose who you want to model and rapidly take on those behaviors and strategies to propel you toward the success you desire.

As mentioned earlier, Sir Isaac Newton once said, "The reason I see so far is because I stand on the tall shoulders of those who came before me." Modeling is a specific tool which, when you really apply it can launch you on to tremendous success. Take the classic book *Think and Grow Rich* for example. Napoleon Hill, on encouragement from Andrew Carnegie, dedicated his life to studying the great players of the time. He modeled their behavior and attempted to unpack their values and their Rule Books so that the information could be synthesized and used by every man and woman willing to heed the signs and play a bigger Game full out. The great news is that with today's technologies and tools you can accelerate that process tenfold. Think of *Three Steps to Wealth and Power* as a modern version of *Think and Grow Rich!*

We have established that your experience of reality is based upon your internal blueprint of reality. You project your reality, and see or experience only that which you are conditioned or taught to look for. You actually live in a quantum soup of pure potentiality, which means you only experience the world that you are conditioned to see until you expand your mind and learn to look through new eyes. Once you do, then you realize that there are other potential realities, other aspects of the Game you could be playing. You are not destined to remain on the same Playing Field unless you choose to. The choice is yours. You can design your own destiny.

The best way to learn a new aspect of the Game or to improve your ability to play your current Game is to seek out those who have already mastered it, find out how they did it, and follow in their footsteps. This is the natural process known as role modeling.

Role modeling is something that you have done subconsciously from the time you were born. According to sociologist Dr. Morris Massey this role modeling is responsible for many of your values and beliefs about life. And it is these role-modeled opinions and ideas that form the basis of your Rule Book.

According to Massey, you go through three major developmental stages, which result in the formation of your Rule Book. These developmental stages are:

0-7 years old   - The Imprint Period
7-14 years old   - The Modeling Period
14-21 years old   - The Socialization Period

Ages zero to seven are considered the Imprint Period. During this time you became an almost cookie cutter imprint of your parents. You subconsciously modeled the values of your parents and you emulated them in most every way. Outside influences such as the culture that your family lived in played a role in the development of your values at this early age. There are certain cultural values that are indigenous to the people that live within the culture.

Were you raised with a religious background, and if so what religion? Did your parents care for you exclusively or did you have a nanny? If you had a nanny, what were your nanny's values and attitudes? All of these things contribute to the development of your values at this early age.

In this developmental period, as well as the two that follow, Massey also points to what he calls significant emotional events. These also play a major role in the development of your values. Was there abuse or trauma in your past? What significant events were occurring in the environment around you? A child who grew up during the Great Depression may have significantly different values than someone who grew up during a time of great prosperity within the country.

Ages seven to fourteen are held by Dr. Massey to be the Modeling Period. During this time you began to find role models either inside or outside of the family. Inside the family might include older brothers or sisters. Other children at school and their values also influenced you. You found heroes and were greatly influenced by the values of those heroes. Interestingly enough, the media could have had a major impact at this young age based upon the types of heroes who were portrayed in movies or the personalities of the rock stars that you emulated.

What were your heroes' attitudes? When the James Bond movies first came out, how did the character of Bond effect and shape the values of the young men who looked upon him as a hero? How do some of the rock stars of this generation effect and influence the values of our children? Dr. Massey believes that to a large extent, who you are today and the types of goals you set in life are often a result of the types of heroes you had when you were ten years old!

The last of the developmental periods, as Massey describes them, is the Socialization Period. The Socialization Period occurred between the ages of 14 and 21 when you were in the process of fully integrating values, beliefs, and filter systems into your personality. All of the outside influences including media, family, friends, geography, culture, religion, significant emotional events, etc. will continue to have an effect on the values system that you eventually make your own. It is Massey's belief that in the early 20's the young adult will tend to go through a period of experimentation, often in the college years, and will test out behaviors and ways of viewing the world that will sometimes seem to oppose their values. Once they have done that they will tend to revert back to acting in ways that are consistent with the values they hold intrinsically. Massey states that after this stage, your values will tend to remain the same, potentially only altered in the presence of a significant emotional event.

The next stage 21-35 is the business persona and was defined by William James, not Massey. The first people you worked for may have a big impact on you in terms of your business values and behavior. It is these initial employers that will have the biggest impact on your work ethic.

However, over the last decade my focus has largely been on the study of accelerated human change. And I have several techniques that I teach in my live programs that can assist you in changing your own values at will for the purpose of creating the life you want. This can also be done to a certain extent through studying someone you consciously choose to model and how to do that effectively will be the subject of the next few chapters.

Who you are today is largely based upon the Imprint and Modeling Periods of your youth. These, along with the significant events in your life, determine your internal blueprint of reality. And your internal blueprint of reality determines the Game you are currently playing and the rules you play by.

Role modeling is a natural way for us to learn, yet when we become adults we often stop using it.

INSIDE AND OUTSIDE MODELING

"Microsoft's dominant position arose from an operating system closely modeled on a Digital Research product and the graphical user interface technology invented at Xerox."

~ Martin S. Fridson

There are two types of modeling; inside and outside modeling. Outside modeling is a surface level modeling and is much like imitation. When Elvis Presley modeled the best Blues singers of his time, he simply watched what they did and mimicked it. He did the same thing when he modeled Roy Orbison's vocal qualities. This is the same type of modeling that Greg Luganis did when he was modeling Johnny Weismueller's dives, and the same type of modeling that Rupert Murdoch did with British Tabloid journalism.

Outside modeling can be quite effective, but it is only the tip of the iceberg in terms of powerful modeling. To really grasp the power of modeling it's best to do both. Inside modeling is the process of doing a complete personality profile on the person that you wish to emulate so as to integrate aspects of their personalities into your own. When you do outside modeling you can pick up surface level strategies. When you do inside modeling as taught here, you can actually get the masters' entire hidden Rule Book. This has the potential of accelerating your success a thousandfold. This is the process of taking on their rules for the "Game of Life", as well as expanding your Playing Field by expanding your references.

So if you are currently playing a Game you don't want to play anymore, or playing one badly, wouldn't it make sense to alter the blueprint? Who says that the role modeling you did as a child was all you could do? Who says that you have to accept your lot and be content with survival or mediocrity? Who says that scarcity and failure is part of the program? If these things are in your reality, then someone somewhere told you either verbally or through their actions that this was the nature of the Game. You accepted it. You didn't have to.

Modeling in its simplest form simply allows you access to the tools, strategies, and mindsets of successful people so that you can expand your references and realize how it is possible to play a different "Game of Life" on a larger and more exciting Playing Field.

"Fake it until you make it" is a long held paradigm for success. Far from being dishonest, this principle simply harnesses the power of the mind for accelerated change. Your mind does not know the difference between something that has happened and something vividly imagined. By identifying the new beliefs, values, attitudes, and decisions that have already worked for someone else you get the inside knowledge of the rules by which to play your new Game. Then you can set out to master the same skills and employ the same strategies. You will be well on your way to winning the Game!

Why reinvent the wheel when you can learn from the best of the best? These masters have become so because they have crafted their Rule Book and congruently communicated their vision to the world. They have been clear about who they are, what they stand for and what they want to achieve and have confidently expected to achieve it. You can do the same.

SEVEN

Install Excellence in Yourself Through Speed Modeling™ – What To Do

"I am 15% Phillip Fisher and 85% Benjamin Graham."
~ Warren Buffett

Now that you understand the importance of modeling as a technique to fast-track your success, let's look at exactly how to do it faster than ever before possible. The first step is to find someone who is playing a Game worth playing. Find a role model of excellence. If you choose to model mediocrity, you will end up reproducing mediocrity.

When searching for a role model, ask yourself, "Who is producing the results in life that I want to produce?" Find the person or people who are playing the Game you want to play and study their Rule Book. Learn their rules and incorporate them into your own life. If Gandhi played by the same rules as the rest of the world, he never would have produced the results that he did. If Richard Branson played by the same rules as the rest of the world he never would have become the billionaire he is today.

You need to look at what they are producing and then play by their rules. You need to find out what's going on inside them cognitively that allows them to produce their result. What are the beliefs, values, decisions, attitudes, and other filter patterns that make up their personality?

The best way to model a result is to find the person who is actually producing the result you want and question and observe them directly. A common excuse for not doing this is; "But why would that person speak to me? How could I possibly impose on this person?" Understand you don't have to go to Richard Branson first off. Find someone in your local community that is playing a Game you want to play. Perhaps there is a couple that you know who have a wonderful marriage. Perhaps there is a guy two doors down who religiously works out and has a body you admire. Perhaps there is a marketing award winner at work that you could approach if your ability as a marketer is something you want to improve.

Get creative and ask. I guarantee everyone loves to be admired and all the successful people I have ever approached have been thrilled and excited, that I was interested enough to ask. Everyone loves to share his or her story.

The second best way to model excellence is to compile information from various sources about your subject. Go into your local bookshop and have a look at the biography section. If you can't reach Richard Branson personally, read his biography. Research the person you are interested in through interviews, articles, and television documentaries. You should aim to read at least four to six books on each person you want to model and watch at least four television interviews or programs featuring that person so you can model his or her external behavior and mannerisms. I will show you how to do much of the modeling process very quickly using a master strategy for genius reading. This will allow you to speed through the books with ease.

An accurate model can often be produced from a combination of sources when you don't have access to the actual person. The important thing about the modeling process is to create a useful road map for replicating excellence in any particular Game. Whether or not the model is "real" or "right" is irrelevant. The fact remains that when you follow the model or the Rule Book of this successful person you can learn to produce the same results.

WHAT TO WATCH FOR

In Chapter Six we talked about inside and outside modeling. The quote from Oprah Winfrey, which I will re-quote here, is an example of outside modeling:

> *"When I did my first audition for my first television job, I was such a nervous wreck, I had no idea what to do or say. And I thought in my head that maybe I'll just pretend I'm Barbara Walters. I will sit like Barbara and hold my head like Barbara. So, I crossed my legs at the ankles, I put my little finger under my chin, I leaned across the desk, and I pretended to be Barbara Walters."*

You can isolate the nuances of behavior by watching the person you wish to emulate on television. The biography channel is a great source for this sort of information. Notice the similarities of behavior that are consistent. Like Oprah in her earlier days, notice the little things that make that person different and mimic that. When I first read that quote I thought, "If it's good enough for Oprah, it's good enough for me!"

Then there is the inside modeling, which is working out how that person thinks. Again a great deal of this information can be deduced from interviews and books. For inside modeling the things you need to look out for are all the filters we talked about in Chapter Four.

Values

Values, as mentioned before, are simply those things that someone considers important.

As you begin to study those you choose to model, a major key to reproducing the same result will be to find out what drives them. Richard Branson for example, values "living life to its fullest" and "having fun." He also values "entrepreneurialism" and "challenge."

Oprah Winfrey values "making a difference." Donald Trump values "being tough" and "winning." Celine Dion values "being the best." Values sculpt the Game you play. When you are modeling an individual, his or her values will be revealed through their personal descriptions of life, their passions and how they spend their time.

Beliefs

Beliefs form the rules in your life. Rupert Murdoch, primary shareholder of News Corporation and one of the most powerful men on the planet, was quoted during his rise to the top as having said, "There is no question that we will be successful. The only question is what level of success we will attain." This belief supported his success and propelled him forward.

Oprah Winfrey has repeated on numerous occasions her belief that, "Excellence is the best deterrent to racism and sexism." This belief has allowed her to excel where others chose mediocrity.

Warren Buffett has a belief that it's easier to create money than to spend it. John D. Rockefeller had a belief that "the power to make money is a gift from God." Both have created phenomenal wealth! A person's beliefs can be heard in what they say and for that reason quotes are a great place to find beliefs. You can also ask yourself the question, "What are the underlying assumptions about their capabilities and the world that are revealed through their statements?"

Decisions and Decision Points

Your decisions determine your destiny. In fact, in my modeling of extraordinary men and women throughout time, one thing I have discovered is that they really weren't extraordinary at all. They were simply ordinary people who made extraordinary decisions about the events in their lives.

When Nelson Mandela was in his teens, he was attending a traditional ceremony within his tribe that signified his passage into manhood. After the ceremony, one of the tribal elders stood up and said, "These are our young men. They are our pride and joy. They are our future. But the truth is that they are not men at all, and in fact they will never be men. Our land is not our own. They are second-class citizens in their own homeland. They are boys, not men, and they will always be boys." When Nelson Mandela heard those words, he made a decision to change the political face of South Africa. That decision changed his country, and ultimately the world.

When Richard Branson was young he was "branded" dyslexic. For many that label would have served as an excuse for mediocrity and created a limiting decision about what was possible—not Branson. He decided that the dyslexia didn't limit him but rather it made him more intuitive in business because he wasn't adept at reading financial reports. Branson is not the only billionaire to have been told he was dyslexic. So were Charles Schwab, Craig McCaw, and David Murdoch.

It is not the events in your life that shape your destiny, but the decisions you make about those events. These decision points can be found by examining the significant emotional events in their life, and then looking at how those events became turning points. What direction did the individual take as a result of those decision points? What conclusions did they draw from these events? The answers to these questions will give you tremendous insight into their thinking.

Attitudes

Attitudes are abstract filters of perception that are a combination of beliefs and values around certain subjects. What attitudes does the master exhibit? Are they easy-going? Are they fun-loving? Are they friendly? Are they tough? Are they committed? Are they resilient? Are they frugal? Warren Buffett, Donald Trump, Bill Gates and Richard Branson, all multi-billionaires, have all been described as being "obsessed" with expansion and highly focused as a result. Trump, as well as Buffett, despises imbecility and incompetence. On the flip side of the coin, Buffett is well-known for his good-natured and fun-loving attitudes about life.

META PROGRAMS

When you are studying a master of the Game you choose to play, study their Meta Programs, and then you can choose to take on the same patterns. You'll recognize these patterns from the introspective test you took in Chapter Four.

Motivation Filter

Does the individual you are modeling move primarily in the direction of what they want in life, or "away from" what they don't want. Once again, the person who moves "toward" what they want is motivated by concepts such as, achievement, recognition, or freedom; whereas the person who is primarily "away from" motivated is more concerned with things such as: not wanting to be broke, or fear of never being "somebody." The motivation filter has everything to do with how we focus on goals.

Our focus is made up of six things: pictures, sounds, feelings, tastes, smells, and self-talk. These are all of the things that we can do inside our mind and bodies. The question is, when the person you are modeling focuses on their goals, are they making pictures, sounds and feelings of great success in their mind, or are they making pictures, sounds, and feelings of *not wanting* poverty and lack?

This filter, as with several others, could be context dependent. Perhaps the person is "toward" motivated in their career yet "away from" motivated in their health.

You may find that the person you are choosing to model is any of the options below:

- Toward motivated
- Toward with a little away
- Both toward and away equally
- Away with a little toward
- Away from motivated

When you understand how those you most want to emulate motivate themselves in those areas where they are successful you can choose a similar strategy. My prediction is that in the areas of their lives that they have consistently working for them, they will be "toward" motivated and in the areas of their lives that either aren't working or where they have inconsistent results they will be "away from" motivated.

Here's a perfect example of what I'm talking about. Oprah Winfrey has a certain area of her life that has consistently worked for her, namely, her career. There are other areas where her results have been less than consistent, such as managing her weight. Now, I admire Oprah tremendously and she is an example that most everyone is familiar with so she's a useful topic for illustration. She did an interview on America Online where she was asked what motivated her to work, and she responded, "to work or to work-out?" The interviewer laughed and Oprah continued, "If you want to know what motivates me to work it's this... I am on a mission. You see I feel that if I can assist people to take responsibility for their own lives, we can change the world... Now if you want to know what motivates me to workout, it's because I don't want to have a fat butt!"

The "toward" motivation of her career produced consistent, extraordinary results. The "away from" motivation of her health and fitness produced inconsistent results. The first step to taking charge of your motivation direction is to set lofty "toward" goals. We teach in-depth methods for taking total control of your motivation direction in some of our live seminars. However, recognition of the pattern is clearly the first step.

Orientation Filter

The person who is possibility oriented will think of all the possibilities in life, whereas the person who is necessity oriented may focus on their obligation and be moved to action by these obligations. Which of the following is the person you are modeling oriented toward?

- Possibility
- Necessity
- Both

Martin Luther King was someone who operated primarily based on the possibilities available until he became a reluctant hero and stepped up out of obligation and necessity to champion his cause. He later shifted back to possibilities, so King could be considered both possibility and necessity. As you study the individuals you model notice *why* they do what they do.

Success Indicator Filter

How does the person you wish to model evaluate their performance? Do they look for external verification of how they are doing, or do they just know inside themselves how they've done? Are they more concerned with what others think about them, or with what they think about themselves?

Warren Buffett once said, "I keep an internal scoreboard. If I do something that others don't like but I feel good about, I'm happy. If others praise something I've done, but I'm not satisfied, I feel unhappy." Obviously, Buffett uses an internal success indicator. Those you are modeling will tend to fall into one of the four categories listed below:

- Internal
- External
- Internal with external check
- External with internal check

Decision-making Filter

This filter determines how someone makes a decision. Do they see something that convinces them, do they have to hear it, read about it, or do it? Guess which filter Warren Buffett uses—he once said, "In the end, I always believe my eyes rather than anything else."

In order to discover this filter, simply look for how the people you are modeling interact with the world and notice what their preferred means of gathering information for decision-making is.

- See
- Hear
- Read
- Do

Convincer Filter

This filter determines how many times someone needs to run through a decision-making process before they are convinced of anything. We all have subconscious strategies for making decisions. This is simply an order and sequence of steps that need to occur in order to make a decision. How many options does someone have to look at or consider before they can make a choice. For some people the decision is made immediately, some prefer to consider a couple of options, others require a certain period of time before they can make a decision and some need to be consistently convinced.

When you examine someone like Richard Branson of the Virgin Companies it's very clear that he has an automatic convincer. He will jump into new business ventures simply because they appeal to his sense of adventure and they sound fun. He has tended to act on things without comparing options and let those around him clean up any mess that is left in his wake, especially in his early days. Warren Buffett on the other hand can appear to be automatic, because he can make decisions very quickly. However, Buffett's seemingly automatic nature is created through his consistent results. His knowledge and experience have taught him to recognize the best deals. Buffett says that he doesn't look for seven-foot bars to jump over, but rather the one-foot bars he can step over. By looking at every option consistently, he can pick the best option automatically.

The people you are modeling should fall into one of the four categories listed below:

- Automatic
- A number of times
- A period of time
- Consistent

Leadership Filter

This filter tells us if the individual knows what needs to be done in order to be successful and also whether they are able to direct others in that process. Are they only able to see what they need to do? Do they know what they need to do but are not great at delegating to others? Are they equally good at both? Do they have no idea what they need to do, but can easily see what others need to do?

Leaders will more often than not be "self and others." It is possible for someone to be in a leadership position who simply attracts others to them to play the role of director, while the leader themselves simply becomes the icon or figurehead, although generally the leader will need both skills.

When you are modeling, notice which category they fall into:

- Self only
- Self and others
- Self but not others
- Others only

Energy Direction Filter

This filter determines how much energy someone will put into pursuing their life goals. People will either be active or reflective in life. The person who is at the far extreme of activity, will take massive action toward their goals, where as the reflective person will tend to do a detailed study of all the consequences of action before doing anything. And the inactive person simply reflects, but never acts. Arnold Schwarzenegger said, "Seek out failure. The confidence and satisfaction of stepping over your supposed limit is enormous." The way he directed his energy makes him "active."

Most successful entrepreneurs will tend to be very active in their approach to life, although they may learn from experience to reflect more before jumping in head first. Investors will tend to be more reflective, but can learn from experience to be more active, as they train themselves to know and recognize value.

- Active
- Reflective
- Both
- Inactive

Performance Filter

Does the person prefer situations in which they are a solo

player, do they prefer to be part of a team, or do they prefer to lead a team? This is different from the leadership filter in that it refers more to where someone performs the best, and therefore gains their greatest pleasure.

Warren Buffett demonstrated his independent and management performance style when he said, "My idea of a group decision is to look in the mirror." Celine Dion is an independent player as was Elvis Presley, whereas their managers, Rene Angelil and Colonel Tom Parker respectively, were management players. Where do the individuals you are modeling really shine?

- Independent player
- Team player
- Management player

Work Satisfaction Filter

Is the person more inclined to work with things, systems, or people? Donald Trump is interested primarily in working with things—the buildings he creates, the worldly trappings of success, and the deals he makes. The Dalai Lama gains satisfaction primarily working with people. What are your role models most interested in working with?

- Things
- Systems
- People

Preferred Interest Filter

What does someone care most about? The people they spend time with, the places they go, the people they meet, the things they have, the activities they take part in or the information they learn? This filter is made clear through the individual's words and descriptions of life. Where do they place the most focus and energy?

Multi-billionaire Ted Turner was very much an activity person throughout most of his life. When questioned early on about his priorities he responded, "They are sailing, business and family, in that order." While his views have changed since then, looking at an individual's primary interests throughout the course of their life can be quite revealing. Warren Buffett's primary interest in information and things has provided him with the natural ability to value businesses and make brilliant purchases.

Preferred interest categories include:
- People
- Places
- Things
- Activity
- Information

Abstract/Specific Filter

Does the individual think in abstract concepts or specific details? The abstract thinker is the person who sees the big picture. The entrepreneur is often an abstract thinker, as is the general in the armed forces. The janitor or the foot soldier thinks in specifics. It is important for people to have the ability to move throughout the range of thought from abstract to specific in order to function effectively in the world.

Donald Trump has been quoted as stating, "If you're going to be thinking anyway, you might as well be thinking big." He grasps the big picture first, yet, he is able to chunk down to the most minute details, such as the cost savings of putting only two hinges on each door rather than three when building a hotel.

How do those you are modeling best grasp and assimilate information?
- Specific
- Abstract
- Specific to abstract
- Abstract to specific

Comparison Filter

This filter relates to how someone views their world. Do they look for the similarities in things or the differences?

Warren Buffett is clearly a sameness person. He drinks the same Cherry Cokes day in and day out, he invests in companies he expects to hold onto for life, he even tends to eat the same types of foods. He once had lunch with Marshall Weinberg of the brokerage firm Gruntal and Co. who remarked, "He [Buffett] had an exceptional ham and cheese sandwich. A few days later we were going out again. He said, 'Let's go back to that restaurant.' I said, 'But we were just there.' He said, 'Precisely, why take a risk with another place? We know exactly what we're going to get." Richard Branson on the other hand falls more into the category of difference with exceptions. He loves to launch many different businesses because the variety is important to him.

What category do the people you're modeling fall into?
- Sameness
- Sameness with exceptions
- Sameness with differences equally
- Differences with exceptions
- Differences

Challenge Response Filter

Does the individual whom you want to model tend to let their feelings run their life or are they more dissociated in their approach toward life? Another possibility is that, under pressure the individual could choose the most appropriate and effective response depending on the situation.

The way to discover someone's challenge response is to simply observe them in a stressful situation. Notice their reactions. They should fall into one of the three below:
- Thinking

- Feeling
- Choice

Time Awareness Filter

Does the person in question map out their time or take each day as it comes? The "through time" person will tend to be very time conscious. This person will tend to know what they will be doing each hour of the day. The "in time" person, on the other hand, will be more interested in living in the moment. They have less direction and care more about fully experiencing the now. Again using Warren Buffett and Richard Branson as examples, they are through time and in time respectively.

- Through time
- In time

Focus Filter

This final Meta Program relates to whether a person is primarily focused on themselves or other people. Are they self-absorbed or is their attention outwards? Mother Theresa was clearly others oriented while Madonna at the far opposite of the extreme was self-oriented, especially in her early years. Ted Turner was very self oriented early in life then moved more in the direction of others later in life. What type of person will you want to emulate in this area?

- Self
- Others

Those are all of the Meta Programs. Here are the rest of the Internal Filters that shape your experience:

LANGUAGE

What sort of language do they use? Are there any words that they use more than average? If you want to model a successful stockbroker, for example, you will have to learn the language of that world. You will have to understand what a PE ratio is or how to read a price bar. Listen to the language and learn it.

Master communicators use language to pull others into their vision and create momentum towards their future. For example, President Bill Clinton used the word "we" 208 times in his last state of the Union Address.

Warren Buffett recognized the importance of this aspect of success when he said, "You should have a knowledge of how business operates and the language of business, some enthusiasm for the subject and qualities of temperament, which may be more important than IQ points. These will enable you to think independently and to avoid various forms of mass hysteria that infect the investment makers from time to time."

MEMORIES AND REFERENCES

Biographies are great for researching memories to see how the individual evaluates their world. When you research the memories and references of someone you wish to emulate, you will automatically expand your own references. This type of exploration allows you to see new possibilities that were previously hidden to you.

Donald Trump once said that by the age of sixteen he knew everything there was to know about building without ever taking a class. His father was a very successful builder and Donald was able to soak up information, which provided him with the reference experiences that would propel him to fame and fortune. This is also why Donald Trump can rebuild so quickly when things go wrong; he's been there before so he knows how to recover based on his references. If you don't have the references to create what you want in your life, you've got to "borrow" other people's references. So study them, as it will expand your own references. At an early point in Oprah Winfrey's career, she had the opportunity to visit Stephen Spielberg's production studio Amblin Entertainment. Seeing this example of possibility expanded her references and she told herself she could create the same thing. This reference experience led her to then create Harpo Productions.

TRAITS

You can often discover traits of a master by researching descriptions of how they interact with others and the world around them. Rupert Murdoch has been described throughout his life as being "very inquisitive," and having an insatiable appetite for learning more about those things important to his business. Celine Dion has been described as being "extremely disciplined." She is possessed by her passion to perform. Madonna was often described during her rise to the top as being "outspoken," "brash," "assertive," and willing to do anything to become a star. Sam Walton of WalMart fame had intense drive and competitiveness. Adopt those traits that you discover in your role models and you too can then produce similar results.

SKILLS AND SKILLSETS

Gandhi was a skilled communicator, as was Martin Luther King Jr., Barbara Streisand worked to develop her comic timing and became known for that in addition to her singing and acting talents. Richard Branson has tremendous leadership ability and is known for inspiring people to move toward a shared vision. Virtually every multi-billionaire and activist I have studied has been an extraordinary sales person. They are adept at selling their ideas, which you'll learn in Step Three!

Once you've identified the skills and skillsets of the masters of the Game, you can commit yourself to perfecting those same skills and skillsets. This tells you exactly where to apply your energies.

STRATEGIES

Strategies are the specific internal or external processes the masters do that allow them to arrive at certain results. There are three different types of strategies that you can elicit when doing inside modeling. These include: micro, macro, and meta-strategies. Micro-strategies are the exact order and sequence of steps that the master of a particular game runs through in order to produce a specific result. Most micro-strategies will be run within a matter of seconds. People have micro-strategies for virtually everything that they do, including love, wealth, poverty, depression, learning, happiness, etc. Eliciting micro-strategies can give you extremely precise information about how to replicate a given result. We cover micro-strategy techniques in depth in some of our live trainings.

Macro-strategies are primarily what you will be looking for after you have read this book. They are general things that someone does in order to produce a certain result. For example, you could examine the leadership strategies of Richard Branson and you might find that he does several things, which when emulated could allow you to produce similar results. This includes: looking to make a difference through his companies, allowing people within his organization to constantly reinvent themselves in order to keep them engaged, and fostering an entrepreneurial mindset within the people around him in order to get many great minds moving together toward the accomplishment of the corporate objectives. (We will cover this particular leadership strategy in Step Three.) All of the above mentioned activities would be considered macro-strategies.

And finally, meta-strategies are simply overall philosophies that cause them to choose all of the other strategies. Meta-strategies can be gleaned by paying attention to the master's driving force in life, as well as their philosophy about business or life in general.

While micro and meta-strategies are both important, macro-strategies are where you will be placing most of your focus when you begin learning how to model. Be on the look-out for those things that your chosen role model does to create consistent results. For example, Rupert Murdoch manages his many companies by reading what he calls his "blue book" on a weekly basis. The "blue book" is simply a description of every financial inflow and outflow from each individual business. This allows him to keep his finger on the pulse of the entire organization and predict cash flow.

Bill Gates has had a consistent strategy of getting his products to market first before any of his competitors, even if it meant sacrificing some quality. He would then use the general public as his quality control system by fixing software problems as they were reported. Warren Buffett purchases companies with top-notch management already in place, rather than turning around companies that aren't working or building from the ground up. Donald Trump has had a strategy of purchasing distressed properties when the owner has to sell and turning them into luxury properties under the Trump name. Arnold Schwarzenegger has had a strategy of seeking out mentors and then surpassing their achievements. Virtually every billionaire I have studied has a strategy of keeping an extremely tight lid on expenses while maximizing revenue. Many actors and actresses, who are successful, including Oprah Winfrey, Matt Damon, Ben Affleck, and Pierce Brosnan amongst others, started their own production companies rather than wait around to be cast in roles.

Arnold Schwarzenegger revealed one of his macro-strategies for achievement when he was recently asked in an interview in the Men's Journal, "You've got money, fame, a great young family. Why take on governing the state of California? What drives you to constantly reinvent yourself even at this stage in your life?" Schwarzenegger responded, "It's not even really a matter of my choosing to make big changes in my life. It's like I get this vision without me controlling it of what I'm supposed to do next, and then that vision consumes me. It becomes me. And from the beginning I absolutely believe that I can do it, you know? It's almost like you have faith that you can do this thing and then you can't wait to get started on what you have to do to get there."

Learn the strategies of the masters and you are on your way to quickly mastering your chosen Game.

EIGHT

Install Excellence in Yourself Through Speed Modeling™ – How To Do It

"Jesus gave me the message,
Gandhi gave me the method."
~ Martin Luther King Jr.

Prior to being imprisoned for twenty-seven years on Robbin Island, Nelson Mandela played the extreme role of a radical activist. His role models had been revolutionaries and guerilla leaders. While he was in prison he made a conscious choice to model himself after individuals impacted the world in more positive ways. Instead he began to read books on individuals such as Gandhi. Nelson Mandela, through his actions and his vision of a free people, led a nation out of apartheid. He spoke of this vision in his Nobel Peace Prize address when he said,

> *"The value of our shared reward will and must be measured by the joyful peace which will triumph, because the common humanity that bonds both black and white into one human race will have said to each one of us that we shall all live like the children of paradise."*

He later went on to say,

> *"We live with the hope that as she battles to remake herself, South Africa will be like a microcosm of the new world that is striving to be born."*

This conscious choice to model different leaders not only molded Nelson Mandela's values, but the face of the nation around him. Another powerful leader, Martin Luther King Jr., at an earlier stage in his personal crusade made a similar choice and it changed him too, then our world. It can do the same for you. Learning from others is an invaluable tool.

If you are unable to meet the person you wish to model face-to-face, the next best thing is to collect a body of knowledge about that individual and begin to extract the most pertinent information for mastering that particular Game. This chapter will teach you how to speed model.

Speed Modeling™ is comprised of three major components: Genius Reading, Mind-Mapping and Cognitive Profiling. These will be detailed in the pages that follow. There are two things you will need to do in order to prepare for Speed Modeling™. The first is to gather information; the second is to learn to access a state of mind known as "expanded awareness."

FIRST – GATHER INFORMATION

First, the question is, who do you want to model? The first step is to gather information about the person you most want to speed model. Six books on each individual being modeled is a good number. This will give a complete picture and varied perspectives.

If your goal is to increase your wealth for example, you might choose someone or a small group of individuals who have amassed a fortune, preferably within your chosen field. If you have yet to decide what field is important for you to make your mark in, then you may choose to simply place your focus on individuals who have produced most of the results that you want, and let your vision of a chosen field be revealed to you as you expand your references through the modeling process. The key here is to listen to your heart and discover what "sings to you" most. If your goal is to powerfully shape an organization or to move the hearts and minds of the people around you, you may choose to begin to collect books and other relevant information on people like Bill Gates or Anita Roddick, creator of the Bodyshop stores. If your goal is to find nirvana and live in inner peace, collect books on those who have achieved that goal. The sky is the limit. It's your world so play the Game you want to play.

And remember that our goals are not exclusive. You might choose to learn the enlightenment strategies of the Dalai Lama and the wealth building strategies of Bill Gates! It's up to you.

Once you've amassed your body of knowledge on your chosen person, it's time to extract their Rule Book…

SECOND – LEARN TO ACCESS EXPANDED AWARENESS

Expanded awareness is a state of mind that is also known as "the learning state" because it creates a mental condition of both total focus and receptivity to new information. I have detailed the steps to being in expanded awareness on the following pages, so that you can rapidly increase the amount of information you take in through your genius reading. Expanded awareness is extremely effective for accelerative learning as it will cause you to be fully present in a state of "uptime awareness." While you are in expanded awareness, it is very difficult for the mind to wander, which in turn causes a heightened state of focus.

There are two types of vision—foveal and peripheral. Foveal vision, also known as tunnel vision, is when you are focused in on something specific. Peripheral vision is when you are looking at the wider or "full" picture.

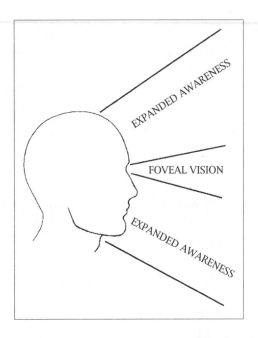

In the context of presenting, we have all seen people who are speaking to groups focus in on one single person for an entire presentation to the exclusion of the group or classroom, yet they are addressing the group verbally. This is an example of foveal vision. Peripheral vision is casting your gaze over the entire group as if they were being addressed collectively or as one entity.

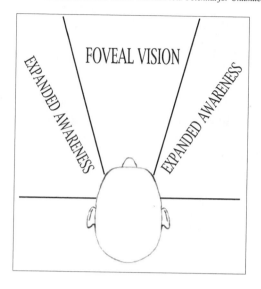

The easiest way to differentiate between foveal and peripheral is to do a simple exercise where you pick a spot on the wall somewhere above eye level. Stare at the spot exclusively and you will be using your foveal vision. Once you've done that for a moment and experienced what it's like to only be using your foveal vision, the next step is to continue looking at the spot, but begin to allow your vision to expand outward into the peripheral. Notice that you can begin to take in whatever there is to see at each side of the spot, and allow your vision to expand as far outward to the sides as possible. All the while you're still looking at the spot, allow your awareness to begin to shift to the peripheral part of your vision.

Then, allow *all* of your awareness to be anchored in the peripheral while still looking at the spot on the wall. Place *all* of your attention in the peripheral.

Once you've experienced that, you can then bring your eyes down from the spot, yet make sure that you keep *all* of your awareness in the peripheral. This seemingly simple technique will prove invaluable in your personal and professional development as you make it a habit to be in that state of expanded awareness.

Now that you have experienced being in this optimal learning state, it is time to get an overview of Speed Modeling™. The process of genius reading, which is the first major component of Speed Modeling™, will require the use of this expanded awareness.

HOW TO EXTRACT ANYONE'S HIDDEN RULE BOOK THROUGH SPEED MODELING™

    A) Genius Reading
        Step 1: Center and clarify your intention
        Step 2: Overview
        Step 3: Expand awareness and mentally photograph 2 pages at a time
        Step 4: Expand awareness and scan each page
        Step 5: Speed read
    B) Mind Mapping
    C) Cognitive Profiling

A) GENIUS READING
Step 1: Center and clarify your intention

Once you have chosen the books, which will give you the vital information about the person you want to model, make sure that you are in an environment free of distractions. The key to effective Genius Reading is focus. Clear your mind and clarify your intention. In the case of extracting someone's hidden Rule Book, your intention is to identify the building blocks of that Rule Book. You'll want to discover specific values, beliefs, decisions and decision points, Meta Programs, strategies, traits, skills, attitudes, etc. Clarifying your intention is simply being clear about what you wish to gain from reading the book. This activates the Reticular Activating System, which will then sort for specific information. Direct your attention to the necessary information so you meet your objective or intention.

Step 2: Overview

The next step is to overview the whole book. Start by normally reading the back cover and inside jacket of the book. Then read the table of contents and the introduction. Once you've done that go into the expanded awareness state and rapidly take in the entire first page. It's best to do this in four seconds or less. Simply scan the page from top to bottom. Do not allow your eyes to focus on individual words, but rather both sides of the individual page and entire groups of words as you glide down the page. Then turn twenty pages or so and do the same thing with the twentieth page. Continue through to the end of the book rapidly scanning only every twentieth page or so.

Your goal here is to get a sense of the author's style and main concepts of the book. When you reach the end, rapidly read through the entire index and bibliography again noticing any keywords that jump out or carry significant meaning.

All of step two can be accomplished in fifteen minutes or less, depending on the length of the book. The more you practice Genius Reading and the more you begin to trust the process, you will find that your speed will increase significantly.

Step 3: Access expanded awareness and "soak in" two pages at a time

The next step is to go into expanded awareness and "mentally photograph" the entire book rapidly. Open up to the first page and visually take in two pages. It will be as if you are mentally photographing each set of two pages at once this time. Your peripheral vision should expand to the point where you can see the sides of each page as if looking at the entire picture of the open book. Do not concern yourself with consciously understanding what is written at this point. Simply trust that your subconscious mind is absorbing everything easily.

There are two things to keep in mind at this stage of the process: rhythm and suggestions. You want to make sure that you continue turning the pages at a steady rhythm, pausing on each set of pages only long enough to take a mental snapshot of each set while in the learning state. While you are turning the pages, rhythmically you can also give yourself positive suggestions such as, "Relax. It's all going in, storing the material at the subconscious level. I'm getting everything and I'll recall it easily." You should be able to complete all of step three in twenty minutes or less, with your goal being to increase your speed as you start to trust the process.

Step 4: Access expanded awareness and
absorb one page at a time

Once you've mentally photographed the entire book, the next step is to go back into expanded awareness and go through the book again this time a single page at a time. Part of what really makes this process work is repetition. Repetition causes the information you are seeking to make a deeper impression at the subconscious level, and therefore increases retention and integration of the material. Start with the back cover again and rapidly scan down it. Then scan the inside jacket introduction, table of contents, and each page of the book. At this stage in the process you may find that certain components of the individual's Rule Book begin to present themselves to you. You may notice, for example, certain traits, beliefs, values, or strategies. As you notice these things you can slow down your scanning and make notes in the margins of the book. For example, if you were modeling Warren Buffett you might find a section in the book where the author is describing him as curious, in which case you could make a note in the margin that says, "*Trait—curiosity/How can I take on this same ferocious curiosity in my own life?"

It's nice to add questions to anything you mark out in the margin because your mind responds to questions and your subconscious mind will work behind the scenes to come up with answers. Your mind is the most powerful computer that has ever existed and if you ask the right questions, it will find powerful solutions.

All of step four can be completed in thirty minutes or less when you are first learning. Once you have completed step four you may want to take a break, perhaps even overnight to allow your subconscious mind to process the information and begin to make new connections.

Step 5: Speed read line by line

Speed read the entire book again, this time line by line. Speed reading is simply rapidly going through every line of the entire book starting with the back cover, table of contents, and each page in order. You can use your finger to guide you and you should be able to go through the entire book this way in the beginning in less than forty minutes, always with the goal of increasing speed as you advance in you ability.

You may find that you have a sense of familiarity with the information because it is the fourth time that you subconscious mind is receiving it. In doing this, your brain has now been exposed to new ways of thinking and acting. In reading about the person you've chosen to model and specifically sorting for their hidden Rule Book, your imagination has been led in new ways. You've made new pictures, sounds, and feelings of these strategies, values, beliefs, etc., which has awakened your neurology by paving new neural pathways. You are now well on your way to integrating the information at the subconscious level. The next step will continue to deepen those new synaptic pathways or thought patterns.

B) MIND MAPPING

At this point you want to fully activate the right side of the brain and let the filter patterns reveal themselves through the Mind Mapping. You will be extracting and integrating at the subconscious level all the important and applicable information you got from the books you read. This recall can be done after a single book or two to three books. Mind Mapping is a brilliant tool to create and deepen the new neurological connections and crystallize your newfound knowledge in both your conscious and subconscious. You may surprise yourself when you go through this process with how much you remember and know already. Here is what is actually occurring inside your mind and body as you do this process...

The Neurological Effect of Mind Mapping

Your brain has an estimated ten-to-the-eleventh brain cells, or neurons. That's one million million (1,000,000,000,000) neural-connections. According to Dr. Paul Goodwin from Alaska Pacific University, there are ten-to-the-ten-to-the eleventh-power potential neurological connections in your entire body and mind, which is more than there are stars in the sky, more than there are grains of sand on the entire planet. This makes the brain redundant on a scale of ten-to-one and the body on a scale of three-to-one. What that means is that you have ten times the neural-connections in your brain than you will ever use and three times what you are currently using in the rest of your entire nervous system. That's a whole lot of thinking potential in your mind and body. Your whole mind-body system consists mostly of a whole lot of neurological connections that haven't been fired off yet. Those ten-to-ten-to-the-eleventh-power connections could all potentially be transmitting information like a giant data-processing system, if we actually employed them. We don't necessarily employ them with our habitual thought processes. We *do create* more neural-connections while Mind Mapping.

Whenever you have a thought or emotion or simply receive one of the millions of bits of information that assault our senses each moment of everyday, an electrical impulse is fired off in your brain and is directed down a neural pathway. That means that every time you have a *new* thought or think of something in a new way, you establish a new neural-pathway. When you are Mind Mapping, your brain is actually firing off new synapses, making new neurological connections, using more of its varied abilities than if you were just journaling or taking notes. The associative process of Mind Mapping literally mirrors the natural structure of your brain cells, as well as the brain itself–several branches radiate out from a single branch connected to all others. You are accessing more of your own mind's potential by venturing down synaptic pathways as yet untraveled. Your Mind Map will resemble these brain cells:

Habits are actualized neural networks. They are a specific sequence and order of neurons that form a finely grooved road. Once you go down that road once, it's easier to take it the next time because you don't have to use as much conscious effort, until pretty soon, you have had that thought or experience enough times that it becomes completely unconscious. We hardly realize there is any other way to think.

As Tony Buzan describes the process in *The Mind Map Book*, "everytime you have a thought, the biochemical/electromagnetic resistance along the pathway carrying that thought is reduced... the more you repeat patterns or thoughts, the less resistance there is to them... In other words, the more times a 'mental event' happens, the more likely it is to happen again."

A behavioral habit is then formed by only traveling down the synaptic pathways already created as the "path of least resistance." That is what is happening when people feel stuck in their lives. They want to do or think one way, but find that they keep falling back into old patterns. They only have that one option neurologically. If you took the same road to work day in and day out for thirty years, then one day someone showed you a shortcut, it wouldn't take you long before you started using that shortcut. That is exactly what happens when you use Mind Mapping —you expand your brain's capacity, which creates new pathways, which then gives you new options and abilities to produce different results in your life.

The brain's cerebral cortex learns best by using a wider range of its skills. Optimal intelligence and mind-expansion occurs when we use all seven of them together. They include: Language, Numbers, Logic, Rhythm, Color, Imagery, and Spatial Awareness. The reason Mind Mapping optimizes our learning and processing, problem-solving, decision-making, and intelligence is because it uses every brain function simultaneously, as opposed to outlining ideas in a linear fashion, for example with a black pen on white lined paper. Mind Mapping is a completely associative event, which takes advantage of the intrinsic structure of how the brain works naturally—associative, holistic, and tending to look for patterns and completion.

It has been proven that "great minds" like Einstein, di Vinci and even John F. Kennedy, are indeed great minds because they utilized more of this wider range of mental tools. This is what enabled them to achieve such great things and take us beyond where we had been before. They were accessing more of their brains' power by approaching the world in a more comprehensive manner with words, symbols, linearity, imagery, association, analysis, patterns, color, etc. That's why it is an irreplaceable tool to use when modeling. The process itself actually makes your mind greater. It activates the brain on all levels fostering more creative thinking and imagination. It also augments the power to problem-solve, remember, get the bigger picture, and arrive at a solution.

Once you have done your Genius Reading and extracted the essence of the Rule Book, you need to integrate and solidify the new way into your neurology and that is what Mind Mapping does. As you begin your Mind Map, you are now activating all the information you soaked in from the books you read. You are claiming that information as your own and bringing it into conscious awareness from the stores of your subconscious mind. This then activates those new behaviors, thought patterns, beliefs, values, etc. directly into your nervous system. The new pathways codify and integrate to create new choices at the subconscious level. The more you stimulate those new neural-connections with all this new information, the more deeply you are installing them. As you move forward with these new thought patterns, you are paving new internal pathways that will make it possible to create your desired future. So now that you know why it's so powerful, let's find out how to draw a Mind Map.

HOW TO DRAW A MIND MAP

You will need a large sheet of white paper and a dozen or so color marker pens. The process will take about thirty minutes to complete. You don't want to be disturbed because you will be working from your right brain, which is the creative free flowing side of your brain. Interruptions will hamper your progress. So make sure you are relaxed and the phone is off the hook, the children are in bed and no one wants anything from you for the next thirty minutes.

Start by drawing an oval or circle on the left side of a piece of paper and put the name of the person you are modeling inside. Then draw two flowing lines that reach outward from both sides. These lines look like branching roots or angel wings and should be a different colors. There is a specific reason for using colors.

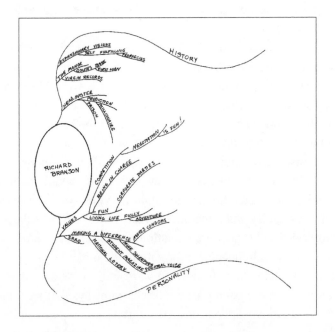

On each of the mind branches you have just drawn you will want to break the individual you are modeling down into two major categories. For example, you could write the word "Personality" on one branch and "History" on the other, or "Strategies" and "Values," depending on how you want to categorize it. Then you create branches that shoot off each wing. On each of the individual branches, you will put subcategories, whatever comes to mind. Put a maximum of three words on each branch. When you are creating subcategory branches, just let your mind run wild. Write down anything you can think of that relates to the book you just genius read and the person you are modeling. There should be little conscious filtering at this point, just free association and creativity. Additional branches can shoot forth from each subcategory branch with additional subcategories.

When you Mind Map you want to be in a flowing creative state of mind. When you are starting to use this process it's a good idea not to concern yourself too much with coordinating colors with categories. In the beginning just allow yourself to associate freely and write down what you remember from the book. Once you become more familiar with using this technique you can ensure that all values are a certain color and all traits etc, are a different color.

Once you have gone through the process, your Mind Map may look something like any of the following:

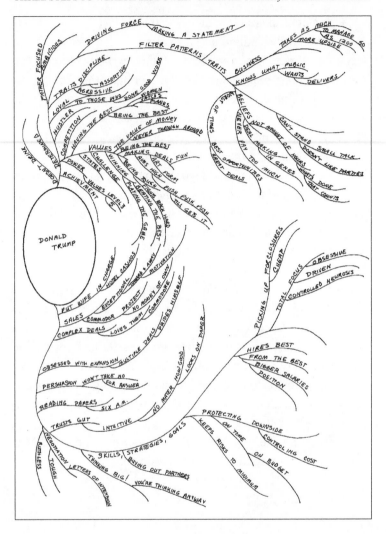

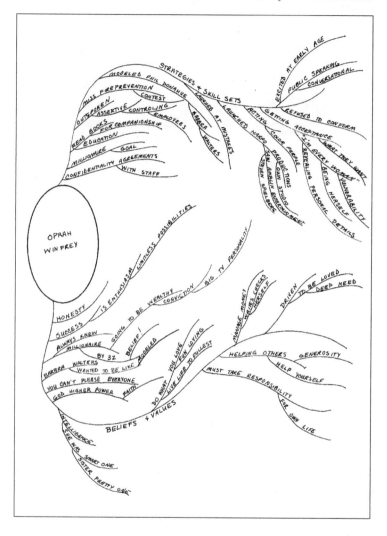

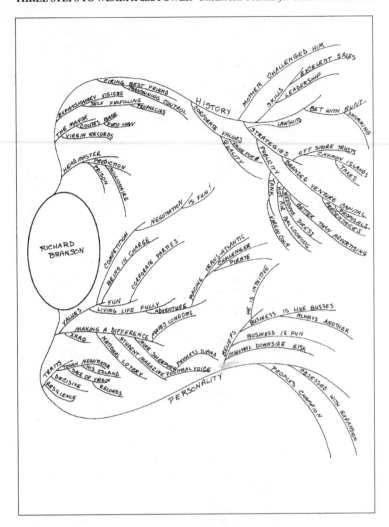

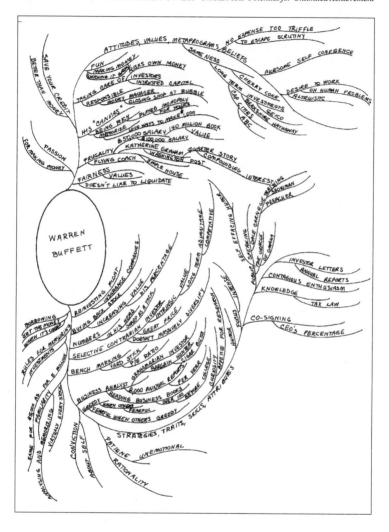

C) COGNITIVE PROFILING

"Employ your time in improving yourself
by other men's writings so that you shall come easily
by what others have labored hard for."

~ Socrates

Categorize your psychological and behavioral map

After you have read somewhere between two and six books on the person you wish to model, and integrated your learning with Mind Mapping, it's time to make a left brain list of each of the major filter patterns of the individual being modeled. To illustrate this process, we will look at the profile of Richard Branson.

Richard Branson

Values

- Fun
- Living life to the fullest
- Challenge
- Competition
- Entrepreneuialism
- Accomplishing "unachievable" goals
- To stand out
- Being the best
- Teamwork
- Making a difference
- Frugality

Beliefs

- Businesses are like busses—there's always another one coming along
- Rules are made to be broken
- Anything is possible
- Negotiation is fun
- Business is creative

- Business is a way of life
- If you go into business just to make money, you're in it for the wrong reasons; it must be creative.
- Every successful business person fails at some ventures
- Business is fun
- Personal relationships are vital in business
- The way to handle a cash crisis is to expand not contract
- Take risks, be bold, but protect the downside
- Needs partners in business to make up for his weaknesses
- He controls his destiny

Attitudes
- Fun loving
- Adventurous
- Life is meant to be enjoyed
- Prepared to try anything
- Live on the edge
- Rebellious
- Enthusiastic
- Politically minded
- Always looking to do anything he can to expand his businesses
- Spends all life working because he doesn't differentiate between work and private life
- Cheeky, humor
- Thrives on opportunity
- Curious
- When told it can't be done, wants to prove them wrong

Meta Programs
- Motivation Filter – Toward motivated
- Orientation Filter – Possibility

- Success Indicator Filter – Internal
- Decision-making Filter – See and do
- Convincer Filter – Automatic
- Leadership Filter – Self and others
- Energy Direction Filter – Active
- Performance Filter – Independent/Management player
- Work Satisfaction Filter – People
- Preferred Interest Filter – Activities
- Abstract/Specific Filter – Abstract to specific
- Comparison Filter – Differences with exceptions
- Challenge Response Filter – Choice
- Time Awareness Filter – In Time
- Focus Filter – Self and others

Language

- "Employees are first, customers second, shareholders third."
- "I don't think of work as work and play as play. It's all living." (Fortune Magazine)
- "It's much more fun in life being the underdog trying to topple Goliath. We've had a lot of fun trying to do things differently than the big established companies who've become a bit fat and gloated… and over charging the customer… and see if we can come in and do it in a way that we can be proud of." (The Biography Channel)

Decisions and Decision Points

- Early childhood experiences with dyslexia made him more intuitive as he couldn't understand numbers and math
- Didn't do well in school and couldn't compete in sports, so he decided he would make his mark in business

Memories and References

- Mother was always thinking of ways to make money
- Brought up with attitude of putting other people first
- Mother always wanted him to be "busy," worked odd jobs, etc.
- Had the experience of being good at sports prior to his injury, so had a reference for excelling at something
- When he left school at age seventeen, his headmaster predicted he would either go to prison or be a millionaire

Traits
- Determined to be the best
- Ambitious
- Resilient
- Ruthless
- Charming

Skills and Skill Sets
- Sales
- Negotiation
- The ability to persuade people to say yes
- Never takes no for an answer

Strategies
- Gets people to reinvent themselves in companies
- Long term financial growth strategies
- Protects downside
- Runs his companies out of houses
- Has Virgin name registered as an offshore trust for tax purposes
- Branded venture capital

Armed with the inside story of what makes a particular person tick and what Rule Book he or she lives by, you expand your references and are able to adopt those traits to assist you in achieving your own success. With the cognitive profile, you have the internal and external roadmap for producing results now far beyond your wildest dreams!

A good thing to do at this stage is to take a look at the skills and skill sets of the person for whom you have just created cognitive profile and rate yourself on a scale from 0-10 in terms of you level of expertise in each of those skills, with zero being "no skill" and ten being "excellent." Then commit yourself to becoming a ten at each of those skills. If you do that, you will rise to the top of your chosen field in no time.

We have covered a great deal of territory up to this point in the book. You are challenged to see that *you* create your own reality. What you create is dependent on a myriad of factors that shape your current life and your future destiny. You have become aware of all those aspects of your thought patterns and belief systems that run your behavior and ultimately your results. Now, you can either choose to be enslaved by them *or* you can harness all the power of that new knowledge. You have the tools to unearth your own hidden Rule Book, not only to understand yourself better, but to understand others better so you can model excellence and change your own course forever. It's like being given a blank canvas for the rest of your life. By knowing what you want to do, you can find others who have achieved what you desire, borrow their paint, and recreate your own masterpiece.

Part three of this book goes on to describe many more of the tools of Creation Technologies™. They are some of the best and most effective techniques to navigate the Playing Field of Life and work in concert with your teammates to win!

Step Three
PLAY TO WIN!

Whether you are playing cricket in Pakistan, soccer in Brazil, or baseball in America, certain skills and attitudes, exercises and training systems have been developed for any player to achieve success, whatever the game. The Game of Life is no different. You must expand your emotional, mental, and physical fitness to perform optimally as a player. Then learn how to work with your team to attain the ultimate prize—winning.

Now that you have awakened to your internal filters and belief systems that have been determining your experience thus far, and you have chosen the Game you want instead, it's time to train in all the skills and techniques that will make the biggest difference in moving you forward to your goal and learn how to work powerfully with your team.

Whatever field you decide to play on, whether you want to be a CEO, an ingenious inventor, or a dedicated parent just remember it is never a completely solo effort. So in this next section you will install the proven strategies, communication, and leadership skills to drive yourself forward and to elicit the cooperation of others in the creation of your dreams.

NINE

Play to Win
An Introduction

*"There are plenty of good ideas if only they can be backed
with power and brought into reality."*
~ Winston Churchill

There are two things that determine our success in life —
1) how and what we communicate to ourselves inside our own
mind and body, which includes how we think; and 2) how we
communicate with other people. Everything we have covered
thusfar was about improving our communication with ourselves.
Much of the rest of this book is devoted to all the ways you can
communicate with others to create synergistic relationships and
inspire others to work together to carry your vision forth and
make it a reality. The question is how do you get ten, twenty, one
hundred, or even thousands of people conspiring for your success?

When Richard Branson was fifteen years old he launched
his first business venture called *Student Magazine*. It was born
out of frustration because he wasn't doing well in school. He
had been branded dyslexic at an early age. So he concluded that
school wasn't going to be the place where he would excel. Due
to a knee injury he also realized that sports could not be his
platform to shine. At this point he could have chosen to believe
his "problems" were going to hold him back for the rest of his
life—but he didn't. Instead he decided he'd make his impact in
business.

He thought there was a niche in the market for a magazine that would air the political views of the student population in Britain. So he founded *Student Magazine*. In order to make it work, he had to sell ad space to fund the venture. In fact, at the beginning he had to sell ad space for a magazine that didn't actually exist. It's easy to look at him now and see his multi-billion dollar empire and assume his level of success is out of reach for you. But Richard Branson didn't build that empire overnight. It was a journey and when you break it down you realize that there were some simple, solid skill sets that went into making it happen.

So here he is, fifteen years old, and he needs to sell ad space to make his vision a reality. He picks up the phone and starts calling every business in town. There is a certain amount of courage that goes into that action as well as a level of communication excellence and negotiation skills, not to mention influence and persuasion. But there is also an ability to convey a vision of something. Having the vision isn't enough. The magicians in the material world are those who can weave the abstract vision, then reach up into the ethers and pull it down with enough specificity to turn it into results.

Branson was able to do that and *Student Magazine* was born. It wasn't a huge financial success, so later in his career when the magazine started to flounder he decided to use the magazine to launch a little mail order record business called Virgin Records and that worked a little better! But he was frustrated at the way the music industry worked because as a retailer of music his ability to make money was capped. He realized that there was more money in the business if he got involved with the musicians themselves and actually cut the records rather than just selling and distributing them.

His next step was to create The Manor, a fifteen bedroom house set in the English countryside where artists could come and record music. This was an ambitious project—fifteen bedroom country houses don't come cheap! Once again he found himself in a position where he had to communicate his dream and sell the vision, this time to investors.

Imagine a young kid in his early twenties walking into the bank and asking for a mortgage on a fifteen bedroom house! Yet he did it. He walked into Coutes Bank and was able to communicate his vision for The Manor so successfully and so powerfully that he persuaded the bank to give him a mortgage.

He then persuaded his parents to kick in another $2,500 and his aunt another $7,500. Suddenly an idea had become a reality. Branson set up The Manor, which launched the Virgin empire we know today.

Warren Buffett, recently voted the most powerful man in the world by *Fortune Magazine*, did the same thing. He is the most successful and richest investor of all time with an approximate $36 billion dollar net worth. When he was in his early twenties, he decided to create his first investment house. He studied what others had done before him, specifically Benjamin Graham. He modeled their methods, their performance and their business and decided to do the same thing himself. Yet he only had $100 of his own money and investment houses required significantly more than that! But Buffett had something far more valuable than money alone—he had vision and passion. He met with significant opposition, yet he was so passionate about his vision for the future that he managed to convince seven people to invest and eventually pulled together $105,000. This was a significant amount of money at the time, considering this was the early forties and he had no track record showing he could actually do what he was claiming he could. Nonetheless, he was able to powerfully convey his dream in such a way that he convinced seven people to believe in him. Getting others to collaborate in your vision is one of the essential keys to success on all levels.

Donald Trump is another example. Trump made his fortune buying distressed properties and turning them into luxury buildings with the Trump name on them. But when he first launched his early development ventures he did it with no track record and little to no money of his own. One of his first development deals was the Commodore Hotel in New York City. When he first announced his intentions, the people around him told him that he was crazy. This twenty-eight year old kid with no record of success wanted to renovate an old seedy hotel and turn it into a luxury property during the height of the city's financial crisis in 1974. In order to pull this feat off, he had to use every communication tool and skill of persuasion in the book. He had to secure 45 million dollars in loans. He had to convince the city to give him a huge tax break, to literally become partners in the project, give up their taxes, and convince Hyatt Hotels to partner with him as well, in order to pull the whole deal together. He convinced the people around him that his vision was worth investing in and sure enough, he was right. Donald Trump went on to make a fortune.

I look at all those stories and the results they achieved not just in terms of the money they made but in terms of the results they were able to create in the world around them. These powerful individuals were able to act effectively in order to get things done. They all thought outside the box of conventionality and then created outrageous dreams by selling these dreams first to themselves and then to those around them. That is my definition of power and influence.

As we travel through the last section of this book, I will be sharing some of the specific techniques these great leaders and others like them have used to achieve their success. Taken on their own they are powerful, used together they are exponentially so. Don't be fooled by their relative simplicity. Sometimes when we start to talk about specific techniques such as rapport building or techniques for being charismatic, we lose the value of the technique because our sights are on the technique not the result, like features versus benefits in sales. The true benefit of learning this information is not the technique itself, but rather the metamorphosis they are capable of producing. These techniques harness your powerful natural ability to influence yourself, your life, and those around you to achieve extraordinary results. Using and mastering the techniques translates into you becoming more magnetic, more charismatic, and consequently more powerful so that you can bring people together to create true win-win situations for all involved. You will be able to control and direct your own destiny and lead the hearts and minds of the people around you in such a way that you produce results that are a hundred times greater than your own individual capacity to produce results.

J. Paul Getty once said, "I'd rather have 1% of the effort of 100 men than 100% of my own efforts." At the time of his death, J. Paul Getty was the richest man in the world and owned a controlling interest in Getty Oil and over two hundred other companies. Through his foundation, he has funded museums and many other art and cultural institutions. He too, knew the power of influence.

The power of influence is, for me, the ability to create a vision in which you fully navigate the Playing Field of life then enroll others in the synergistic pursuit of that vision to create a win-win situation for everyone involved. And the remainder of this book will explore the specific techniques and tools you can employ to do just that.

Let the Game begin!

TEN

Your Road Map to Success: Vision, Mission, Goals, and Values

*"The ability to see and create the future
is the essence of leadership."*
~ The World Future Society

The first step to navigating more of the Playing Field and producing results in your life is to get very clear on what it is that you want. You have to begin taking conscious control of the goals that you set. The more specifically defined your outcome is, the better your chances are of attaining it. Step one and two have been about understanding why you are where you are and learning methods for expanding your Playing Field and changing your destination. The last step is working out where you would rather be and using powerful tools and techniques to get you there as quickly as possible.

I believe we are meant to celebrate the past, and live fully in the now while consciously creating the future. It's now time to take charge and consciously create your future. How do you create something that's not right in front of you, like your present? Begin by determining what exactly your own personal Vision, Mission, and Goals are.

One of the best ways I have found to conceive of such a daunting topic as navigating the Playing Field of Pure Potentiality—your future—is to think of your life as an extraordinary adventure or journey in which you are the hero on your way to fulfilling your ultimate vision.

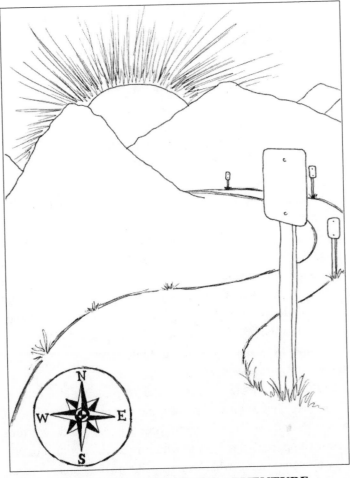

YOUR EXTRAORDINARY ADVENTURE

VISION = SUNRISE

In the picture the sunrise represents your vision, what you ultimately wish to achieve on the horizon. Whether you realize it or not, your subconscious mind has expectations of the future and, as quantum physics has proven, expectations rule outcomes. If you have no expectations, you have expectations of "no." The moment we bring our vision into our conscious awareness it empowers us. The vision can be considered as the ultimate destination. When The Christopher Howard Companies first set our vision statement, and we all conceived it together, it was "By 2005, The Christopher Howard Companies will have assisted over one million people to awaken their potential and lead powerfully effective and fulfilling lives." As this vision came close to fulfillment, we had to write a new vision statement.

MISSION = YOUR PATH

The Mission is the path that you take to get there and how specifically you accomplish that vision. Your Mission is who you are going to be and what you are going to do to reach your Vision. So for example, in the case of The Christopher Howard Companies our Mission is "being the world's leading provider of resources for personal leadership and the expansion of human excellence."

VALUES = COMPASS

Your set of values is your compass. These are the things that keep you true to your path and true to yourself. They will steer the course based on what you believe in, your ethics, and what is most important to you in life. Your compass is critical in getting you to your vision. Values are also extremely helpful when creating a team because a team with shared values is extremely powerful. In some of our certification trainings we teach the process of aligning values within an organization, a couple, or

139

any entity because when people work together holding the same things as important to them, this generates massive propulsion forward.

Those who work with me in The Christopher Howard Companies are all excited about what we do and they want to make a positive difference in other people's lives and have fun doing it. Integrity and pursuit of excellence is also important to me when hiring staff. Because we all have common values, which in turn create synergy and passion, I am confident that together we will achieve the company vision at each stage of our growth. And the same can happen for you, whether you want to transform your existing company, start a prosperous business, provide a happy, loving environment for your family, or create wealth for yourself.

GOALS = SIGNPOSTS

The signposts along the way are the individual goals or milestones that you set. They direct you to your final destination. They tell you when you've taken a wrong turn and guide you back to your path.

A business consultant friend of mine advises that people should set goals for themselves in three-month blocks. It's a highly effective way to manage your time and ensure that you are moving forward. A vision, which at first may seem overwhelming, can easily be broken down into three-month milestones so that the final vision is achieved. It has been said that most of us over estimate what we can do in one year's time and under estimate what we can do in a lifetime. Working in three-month blocks sharpens your focus and keeps you on track.

Take a few minutes now to think about what it is you really want for your life and set your life vision and mission now. When you write these down here, they do not have to be perfect. They are simply meant to provide you with a sense of direction.

For the vision you can simply describe your "perfect day," one you would like to experience at some point in the future. It's remarkable that many people are prepared to spend hours watching T.V., thinking about what to have for dinner, playing computer games, or surfing the internet, yet, they are so reluctant to spend even a few minutes really thinking about their lives and what they hope to achieve. So please, I encourage you to stop for ten minutes and take this first small step toward the future you want and deserve!

This powerful act alone gets your conscious and subconscious mind seeking more of those opportunities that are aligned with your purpose. It will also reinforce to you that you really are the only one creating your unique future and this realization alone can kick-start your future so you can finally start to make your long term goals a reality. Describe it in present tense language but put a future date on it. You can write your Vision for a 5 year, 10 year, or 20 year time frame. When you write your Mission, you will simply want to describe the general path, the vehicle, or who you are going to be such that will lead you to the accomplishment of your Vision.

Remember, your Vision and Mission may very well change over time, so don't get caught up in having them be absolutely perfect now. You will want to review them on a yearly basis and rewrite them as they evolve, or as you find yourself getting clearer and clearer about what you want.

MY VISION IS...

_____

_____

_____

_____

_____

_____

_____

_____

_____

_____

_____

_____

_____

_____

_____

_____

_____

_____

_____

_____

_____

_____

_____

_____

_____

MY MISSION IS…

_____

_____

_____

_____

_____

_____

_____

_____

_____

_____

_____

_____

_____

_____

_____

_____

_____

_____

_____

_____

_____

_____

_____

_____

Once you've written your vision and mission, you have identified the objectives of your personal Game. Next, it's time to create your future and navigate the Playing Field by setting your goals. These goals will act as the signposts on your journey and they will guide you toward your vision. They are your means of keeping score.

> *"It's never been about the money for me. Money is just a convenient way of keeping score."*
> ~ Donald Trump

HOW TO C.R.E.A.T.E. THE FUTURE OF YOUR DREAMS

According to The World Future Society, "The ability to see and create the future is the essence of leadership." This next powerful goal setting tool, called Strategic Visioning™, will give you the ability to see and create your future.

THE "WHAT" IS YOUR JOB, NOT THE "HOW"

When setting goals for any area of your life, the first important question is what you want, *not how* you will accomplish it. Many people prevent themselves from achieving their dreams because they are too concerned with how they could possibly get from point A to point Z.

When John F. Kennedy said that man would walk on the moon during his presidency, they hadn't even developed the technology to make that possible and Kennedy himself certainly didn't know how that would happen. Yet he confidently expected it would happen and on July 20, 1969, the first man stood on the moon. When Thomas Edison set out to create a working light bulb, he did not yet understand the "how." The light bulb was eventually created through massive action and trial and error. As early as the thirteenth century, Roger Bacon said, "Cars can be made so that without animals they will move with unbelievable rapidity." It wasn't until 1769, about five hundred years later, that the first working car was actually built.

The first step therefore is to ask yourself what it is you want, what you ideally want each step of the path to look like. You can't set a course if you don't know where you are going. Without knowing where you're going, you will end up like Alice in Wonderland, feeling lost, wandering without direction or purpose, and depending on others to tell you where to go.

"Would you tell me, please, which way I ought to go from here?"
"That depends a good deal on where you want to get to,"
said the Cat.
"I don't much care where..." said Alice.
"Then it doesn't matter which way you go," said the Cat.

Through your commitment to your vision and mission and through the goal setting you are about to do, you will have taken care of the "what." The "how" will reveal itself to you along the way.

HOW TO SEE AND C.R.E.A.T.E. YOUR FUTURE

Now, let's C.R.E.A.T.E. your goals. The process you are about to learn is the process for getting things in your future so that they actually occur. As management guru Peter Drucker says, "The best way to predict the future is to create it." The process of Strategic Visioning™ which will be described here is something that outstanding achievers do naturally and oftentimes without conscious awareness. Once you learn the process, you can do it anytime you want with volition.

How you write down what you want is very, very important, so as you begin the first step of writing down your goals, make sure your outcomes meet the C.R.E.A.T.E. criteria:

C—Clear and Concise

R—Realistic

E—Ecological

A—As if now

T—Timed and Toward what you want

E—End step/Evidence procedure

C – CLEAR AND CONCISE

It is important that your goal is expressed in a clear-cut, unambiguous manner. It must be specific and concise. If you are writing a financial goal for instance, you want to get specific numbers in the writing of the goal. It's specificity that brings abstract concepts into reality. However, you also want your goal written as concisely as possible. A "nutshell" type statement works best. When your goal is written in a "nutshell" then your subconscious mind, which is the part of you that actualizes goals, can become impregnated with the idea and more easily focus all of its energies on its accomplishment.

R – REALISTIC

Remember, we don't get what we want, we get what we expect. So it's important when writing short term goals to set ones you expect you can achieve. Realistic means achievable to you. If you have never gotten what you want in your life, then scale your goals back by making them more attainable. If you have always gotten what you want, make your goals more grandiose. Stretch yourself. There's nothing that breeds success like success. So it is important that you write goals that you really feel you can hit. There is a tremendous feeling of power that comes with reaching the goals you set. This will breed within you that same empowerment to keep hitting your goals with accuracy and consistency. Once you've created your own track record of success your confidence and expectation in your ability to suc-

146

ceed will expand and you can stretch yourself accordingly.

E – ECOLOGICAL

It is a good idea to run an ecology check on your goals, which simply means looking at the consequences of attaining that goal. Ask yourself, "Is this outcome safe for me, safe for others, and safe to the planet?" Or, "Is this outcome good for me, good for others, and good to the planet?" This thinking allows you to create win-win situations. If you can say yes to all these questions, then you will know it is most likely a good goal to set from an ecological standpoint.

A – AS IF NOW

The reason that we write goals in present tense is that once the mind has fully imagined something, it makes it far easier to accomplish. Because the subconscious mind doesn't know the difference between that which is vividly imagined and that which is real, when you imagine a goal in present tense, as if it were happening *now*, it becomes much more compelling and achievable. So your goal must be written in present tense language as if you are achieving the last step right now in the moment.

T – TIMED AND TOWARD WHAT YOU WANT

Even though you are going to write your goals in present tense, you still must put a date to your goal to indicate when you wish to achieve this outcome. Otherwise it is likely to only exist vaguely off in the future somewhere, in which case it might never even actually occur. It has been said that a goal is a dream with a deadline. The "T" in C.R.E.A.T.E. also stands for "Toward what you want." It's important to express your goal positively, rather than including negative language about what you don't want.

The subconscious mind cannot process a negative statement directly. If I were to say to you, "Don't think of a blue hot-air balloon soaring off into the sunset," you must first imagine it in order to then eliminate the picture from your mind. At best, it's a two-step process. So for example, from a focus perspective you would not write, "I am not fat anymore." You would write, "I weigh 120 pounds and feel fantastic." Because your focus determines your results in life, you want to ensure that your words direct your focus toward what you want.

E – END STEP/EVIDENCE PROCEDURE

This is the difference that makes the difference in this process, as opposed to general visualization. Always include the final end step that lets you know you've really achieved your goal. This is the event, situation, or result that would have to occur in order for you to have attained your outcome. You can also think of this end step as your evidence procedure—how you are going to know when you have gotten your desired goal. Or, what is the last thing that needs to occur so that you know you got it? For example, if you wanted to buy a home, you might write your end step as, "I am signing the papers on my new home," or "I have moved my furniture into my new home," or whatever specific picture you need to prove you have achieved your goal.

I was working with a car salesman who wanted to double his sales. So I asked him, "What's the end step, the last thing that has to happen so that you know you've doubled your sales?" He replied, "I'll be standing in the dealership looking up at the chart on the wall where they post our sales results. I'll see that I jumped from number 26 on the list up to #1 and I'll see that I have X amount of gross sales next to my name." He brought the end step to a level of specificity that caused him to produce that result. Thirty days after our work together the car salesman surpassed his goal, and one year later he was still at number one through consistent use of the Strategic Visioning™ technique.

A simple formula for verifying that a goal you are writing meets a majority of the criteria above is to use this format when writing it:

1. It is now _____ (Future Date)

   I am/I have _____

   _____

   _____

   _____ (End Step/Evidence Procedure)

For example, suppose your goal is to get a pay raise at work. You could write:

*"**It is now**... November 22nd, 2005 at 5:00pm.*
I am... standing in my boss' office shaking her hand.
She has just agreed to raise my income by 10%."

Once you've written the goal, verify that it meets all of the C.R.E.A.T.E. criteria.

> • Your outcome is written in present tense with a future date. "It is now November 22, 2005."
> • It is Ecological. You've asked yourself if the goal is safe to all involved, and you've even determined that it's in the best interest of your company.
> • You have a specific date for the accomplishment of your goal. Putting the exact time of day in there, is optional. Include anything that makes it clearer to imagine.
> • Your goal is stated positively. "She has just agreed to raise my income by 10%."
> • Lastly and most importantly, you have included the end step or evidence procedure for your goal. Remember, this is the last thing that has to happen so that you know

for sure you have achieved your desired outcome. The end step here is the boss shaking his/her hand, having agreed upon the raise.

Now that you understand the formula for writing goals, it's time to implement it.

As you consider your vision in life, now consider some intermediary steps along the way. Ask yourself what would be a good two week goal, one month goal, and three month goal that you could set, which if you hit them would move you closer toward your vision. Taking each goal, create your goal statements now and make sure they meet the C.R.E.A.T.E. criteria.

1. It is now _____ (FUTURE DATE)

   I am/I have _____

   _____

   _____

   _____ (END STEP/EVIDENCE PROCEDURE)

2. It is now _____ (FUTURE DATE)

   I am/I have _____

   _____

   _____

   _____ (END STEP/EVIDENCE PROCEDURE)

3. It is now _____ (FUTURE DATE)

   I am/I have _____

   _____

   _____

   _____ (END STEP/EVIDENCE PROCEDURE)

STRATEGIC VISIONING™ IN YOUR FUTURE TIME STREAM

After having written your goals and checked that they meet the C.R.E.A.T.E. criteria, the next step in the process of Strategic Visioning™ is to get each goal into your future so that they actually occur.

The technique for putting a goal into your future Time Stream is one of the most powerful techniques in existence for producing results in your life. It allows you to literally navigate the Playing Field of life and move from goal to goal with precision and accuracy.

> *"This [Theory of Relativity] required abandoning the idea that there is a universal quantity called time that all clocks would measure. Instead, everyone would have his or her own personal time."*
>
> ~ Steve Hawking

WHAT IS YOUR TIME STREAM?

Aristotle first spoke of the stream of time in Physics IV. Sir Isaac Newton described time in his Principia Mathematica in 1687 where he thought of time as being like a single line or even a railroad track that went on infinitely in both directions. Einstein added to our understanding of time even more when, in his Theory of Relativity, he abandoned the notion of absolute time in favor of the idea that each observer has his or her own conception of time. It proposed that time itself had a shape and it was actually curved in some way. Today we know that people have a way of coding and storing time in their minds and bodies, which is spatial in nature. There was a standard psychological survey done in 1979, titled "*How People Perceive Time,*" in which it was discovered that 99.9% of all the people on the planet have an idea of time that is spatially oriented in relation to their bodies. This is how you know the difference between your memories of an event that happened yesterday and an event that happened ten years ago.

If I were to ask you to just stop for a moment and get a sense of where the past is for you in relation to your body, you might sense, feel, or even imagine that it is behind you, to one side or the other, inside of you, or in any direction in relation to your body. Do that now and point in the direction that seems correct for you. There is no right or wrong answer by the way. Whichever direction it seems to be is just perfect. Do not continue reading until you've pointed in some direction.

Once you've identified where the past seems to be, you can get an idea of where the future is. So once again just stop and ask your subconscious mind which direction the future is for you. It's simply a matter of trusting your intuition. Feel where the future is for you and then point in that direction. Whatever direction you point to is totally appropriate.

Once you have an idea of which way the past is and which way the future is, then imagine where your past and future are connected in a metaphorical line. Some people imagine this line like a "stream of time," or a "strip of film negatives," or like a "chain," or a "string." Notice that the past being in one direction and the future in another implies some sort of line. Once again there are no wrong answers. Your Time Stream is perfect however you perceive it to be. I even had a client, an engineer from Boeing, who imagined his Time Stream as a flat amorphous plane that circled around him.

Once you can imagine your Time Stream in your mind, the next step is to get acquainted with what it's like to rise above it. This entire process is done in your imagination. After all Einstein did say, "Imagination is more important than knowledge."

The greatest accomplishments and the greatest scientific discoveries of all time happened first in the imaginations of those who created them. Einstein himself created the Theory of Relativity by imagining himself sitting on the end of a light beam traveling at the speed of light and looking in a mirror at a clock behind him. He wondered, if he stayed at the front of the light beam traveling slightly faster than the speed of light, would the clock stop or even actually go backwards? The imagination is all powerful and can lead us to places we have never been before. So let's invoke the awesome power of your imagination and do a test drive above your Time Stream. First read the instructions once through, then set the book down in order to do the actual process. I will list the steps first, then further break each one down.

1) **Imagine rising above your Stream of Time**

   Close your eyes and imagine that you can just rise right out of your body and up into the air so that you are in the heavens above this moment now. And as you look down on now, notice that you can see yourself down below and that you can rise up even higher and higher above your Time Stream. Rise so far up that when you look down on now, it seems very small and insignificant. Then observe your Time Stream stretched out in a sort of line with the past going in one direction and the future in the other. Now at this point it's important to realize that this is not only a visual process. Be open to also experiencing the process in feelings and/or sounds. It's all in your imagination, one of the most powerful tools you have. Imagine and pretend to be above the Stream of Time. The experience could be made up of pictures, feelings, and sounds or any combination of the three. However you imagine the process is fine.

2) Imagine stepping back into the past, remaining above your Time Stream, as if you were in the heavens, with the past down below you

Once you have a sense of rising above the Time Stream below you, then simply step back into the past, all the while remaining above the Time Stream.

3) Imagine stepping out into the Future, remaining above your Time Stream, with the future down below you

Once you've gone back into the past, then remain above it and step out into the future.

4) Bring your focus back to now and back into the room

Then come back to now, arriving right back into the room. This entire process should take one or two minutes. Go ahead and do that now…

Great. Now you are familiar with your own personal Stream of Time. This will help you immensely as you begin to learn to navigate your future.

STRATEGIC VISIONING™

I will start by describing the entire process, and then I will give you the steps in a simple format for putting a goal into your future. Read this section through completely before doing the process.

The first thing to do is to read over the goal that you wrote according to the C.R.E.A.T.E. criteria. Then, really imagine yourself at the end step.

This is a key piece. Imagine stepping into that end step scenario. Associate fully in your imagination so that you are looking through your own eyes, not observing yourself from outside yourself. Instead, see what you will see when you're at the end step and you have your outcome. As you do this, listen to the sounds around you when you have your outcome, and feel the feelings of what it is like to know that you can create whatever you want in your world. If you are not sure how to do this, just pretend that it has happened for real. We used to pretend as kids all the time so we know how to do it. You also do it every night when you dream. Once again, your brain does not know the difference between something that happened and something that you vividly imagine so have fun with it and practice being a kid again.

Once you've stepped into it and fully experienced the feelings, then it is time for you to adjust the sensory qualities of the scene. Imagine little knobs at the bottom of a television set. Begin to adjust the qualities like the brightness of the color. If it is a still picture, you can add movement. If it is moving, perhaps you can increase the speed. You want to adjust all of the qualities. What you are trying to create is a feeling of reality in your own body. You can also adjust the sounds. Notice what you say to yourself when you've got your outcome. Maybe you just got that raise and you're saying to yourself, "Yes! I knew I could do it!" And finally, you can adjust the feelings that are present as well. You can just turn the feelings right up, to increase the intensity of the feeling and experience—just like turning up the volume on the television set.

Once you've adjusted the scene to make it the most compelling for you, then you step back out of the picture, or dissociate, but leave your body in the picture, so that you see yourself inside the picture, kind of like a Polaroid snapshot.

This is a very important step. It makes the process far more powerful than simple affirmations or visualization. Most people who visualize their goals remain inside of them. With this process you step out of it so that you see your body in it. This creates tension in your subconscious, like when you stretch a rubber band. This tension or heightened desire will pull you toward the goal. If you fail to do this step, your subconscious mind might think that you already have the goal, and therefore create no tension to propel you toward it!

Once you step out of the picture and you see yourself inside the picture, take that picture in your mind's eye like a snapshot and rise right up into the air above your Time Stream. When you've got the picture in your imagination and you are above your Time Stream, as if looking down from the heavens, you will then energize the picture with all the life force energy that it needs to become real. This is done by breathing your life essence into the picture.

This part of the process may seem a bit esoteric to some people but it is very important, so please just trust the process. You are focusing all of your will or intention on making this happen. Simply imagine that you are holding the picture in your hands if you want or in your mind's eye, as you rise above your Time Stream now and inhale. As you exhale, exhale through the mouth making a "HA" sound and blowing all of the life force energy into the picture. Do this three times total.

Once you have the picture fully energized, you can then step right out into the future above the Time Stream until you arrive right above the date where you said this event would occur. Just trust that you will know where that is, go with your instincts. When you arrive above that date, simply drop the picture right down into the Time Stream and allow it to take its place there, as if your word were law in the Universe. Once you notice that the event has taken its place in the Time Stream, then turn and look back toward the past and notice that all of the events in the Time Stream reevaluate themselves to support this outcome. Everything that had to happen in order for this event to occur rapidly and unconsciously shifts within the Time Stream to lead to the natural occurrence of your goal.

Then, look off toward the future and notice that all of the events in the future also reevaluate themselves in light of this event. This event becomes a cause set in motion that changes your entire future as well. Once you've observed that, just come all the way back to now and back into the room.

To help you remember the steps, they are abbreviated below:

1) Get the end step of your goal in mind
2) Step into the end step. Associate into it, so that you are looking through your own eyes.
3) Adjust the qualities of the scene or the internal representation. Test for feeling of reality.
4) Step out of the picture. Dissociate, so that you see your body in the picture.
5) Take the picture and rise above the Stream of Time.
6) Energize the picture with three breaths.
7) Float out into the future above the future date.
8) Drop the picture down into your Time Stream into the date you specified.
9) Notice the events reevaluate themselves in your Time Stream to support the goal.
10) Notice the future reevaluates as well.
11) Come back to now.

While this process may seem very simple, and perhaps even a little silly I promise you it is the same process I used to turn my life around many years ago and continue to use today. The results you will achieve using this technique will amaze you. Consistent use of the process on different goals will turn you into a master navigator of the Playing Field of life.

Once the goal is written, it shouldn't take more than a few

minutes to do that entire process. I use it before anything that I do in which I have a significant investment in the end result. I taught the process to a car salesman who got so good at using it that he told me he could actually put the name of the person in his future who would buy a car from him each day, even without having met that person yet, and they would show up and purchase a vehicle.

Another woman from one of my seminar programs put a relationship in her future with a man named "Thomas" whom she had never met. Within three months he showed up in her life. Another woman was living in a trailer park, and after putting a new home in her future, one of her clients actually bought a house for her. It is an incredibly powerful process so please don't underestimate it. Don't brush over it because you think you've tried something similar and it didn't work. Strategic Visioning™ has distinctions that make it highly efficient and productive. Use it and use it now. You will be astonished at the results and the speed that you start to see those results.

ELEVEN

The Success Formula of Masters

"Even if you're on the right track,
you'll get run over if you just sit there."
~ Will Rogers

After the initial Strategic Visioning™ process, there are five major keys to producing the results you desire in life. Even if the masters never performed the formalized process of Strategic Visioning™ as you just did, putting goals into the future is an important part of the master strategy utilized by all successful people, whether by Thomas Edison who created the light bulb, Oprah Winfrey who created the number one talk show in television history, Rupert Murdoch who launched News Corporation or Nelson Mandela who helped to liberate a nation.

Here are the rest of the necessary components to realizing your dreams, the Success Formula of Masters:

1) Create the goal in your future (Strategic Visioning™)
2) Take immediate action.
3) Have enough sensory awareness and acuity to know if you are being effective.
4) Have the flexibility to adjust your behavior until you produce the results you want.
5) Utilize everything that occurs to your advantage.

Despite what some well-meaning people say, attaining exactly what we want in our lives is not only about thinking posi-

159

tively. Once you've set your outcome, you've got to do something about it. Ever hear of the husband lounging on the sofa who said to his wife, "I'll think about digging the garden in a little while. Right now I'm thinking about painting the screens." Thinking about painting the screens is still no substitute for painting the screens.

I had someone who was attending one of my seminars approach me and say, "I'm having trouble creating what I want in my business. I've been to all kinds of seminars and I've really got my thinking straight, but I'm still waiting for it to manifest in my life." I said, "Well, I've always been good at manifestation, but I've never waited for it."

You've got to act!

Do *something*—anything! Thought alone will not create the result you want. You have to take action, have enough sensory acuity, and the ability to assess if you are getting the results you want or not. They say the definition of insanity is to do the same thing over and over again and expect a different result. Sensory acuity, which we will talk about in more detail shortly, is having the awareness to monitor the results and make the necessary adjustments so as to fine-tune your actions to ultimately achieve your desired result. You may have to adjust your course slightly as you go and if you stay on course you will arrive at your destination.

If a pilot takes off from New York to fly to Dallas, he or she may be technically off-course several times during the flight. By monitoring the appropriate situation, remaining aware of the flight path, and the relevant dials, the pilot is able to take the appropriate effective action to get back on course and land safely in Dallas.

The way to produce effective and efficient action is to simply embrace steps #3 and #4 of the Success Formula for Masters and repeat them until the result is acheived. They are, once again:

3) Have enough sensory awareness and acuity to know if you are being effective.
4) Have the flexibility to adjust your behavior until you produce the results you want.

It's also very important to use anything and everything that occurs to your advantage as you create your future. The people who are the most successful in life are masters of utilization. John D. Rockefeller once said, "I always tried to turn every disaster into an opportunity."

Donald Trump attended the grand opening of a golf course that he purchased in Southern California. As it began to rain a reporter asked him, "Aren't you upset that it's raining on your opening day?" to which he replied, "Are you kidding? Rain on the opening day always means good luck and success!" He used the circumstances of the moment to his advantage and chose the meaning to support his outcome.

When billionaire Richard Branson was still a teenager and his *Student Magazine* wasn't making money, he used the situation to his advantage by launching a mail order record business through the magazine. The mail order record business was a little company he called "Virgin Records." Later, when the mail carriers went on strike, he opened a store front. This use of circumstances and his willingness to see a different route launched him on a path toward extraordinary financial success.

These are two examples of how utilizing sensory acuity and behavioral flexibility determined these individuals' choices toward success. These abilities can also be applied when making corporate decisions. The best companies in the world use this strategy for success. When Phizer pharmaceuticals was developing Viagra, their expectation was that it would treat chest pains. When it "didn't work," they almost scrapped the entire project. If the researchers and executives had not been able to think beyond their original intentions, they would never have opened up a whole new market, offering new life to an entire population of men and women. The revenues from this "failed" experiment were $788 million within the first nine months it was on the market. Viagra far surpassed sales of Prozac as the most successful drug ever launched. That is called using sensory acuity and behavioral flexibility.

OBSTACLES

The moment we set a goal, we create our own obstacles. Think about it. Before we decide on a goal, there are no obstacles to its accomplishment. For example, say you wanted to attend one of my live programs. Once you have set the goal, you may find that there are some obstacles that arise. You may say "I don't have the money," or "my grandmothers 90th birthday party is on that weekend," or "How will I get there?" None of these considerations were relevant until you created a goal to come to the workshop. Your grandmother's party may have been relevant but it only became an obstacle when the possibility of a conflict arose because you decided to come to the workshop.

The easiest way to avoid obstacles is to have no goals. This is why many people don't even bother setting goals in the first place; they don't want to deal with the obstacles to a goal's accomplishment. The moment we set a goal, the moment we choose the direction, the obstacles become real. Every time you run into an obstacle in the future, you will understand that the very fact that you hit the obstacle means that you are on course to your goal. Then all you need to do is find a way to use that obstacle to your advantage. Have enough behavioral flexibility to think about your situation differently. You may need to take a detour to get around the obstacle, but often these detours are necessary to the journey. So persist. Obstacles are just life's tests to see how badly you want the goal in the first place!

ALWAYS OPERATE FROM A PHYSIOLOGY AND PSYCHOLOGY OF EXCELLENCE

Physiology is important because you must hold yourself in a way that is congruent to your vision. Your physiology must match your statement. You couldn't, for example, be smoking as you announced to the world the imminent launch of a new chain of fitness centers. You couldn't, for example, meekly suggest that this new product you developed is going to change the planet. You have to stand up for what you believe in and put yourself on the line to achieve it. The psychology of excellence is also very important, and again it's about being congruent with your vision and being confident enough to stand up for what you believe in to make it happen.

MOVE CONFIDENTLY IN THE DIRECTION OF YOUR GOAL AND BE KIND TO YOURSELF ALONG THE WAY

One of the most important things that I have learned is to keep moving forward toward my long-term vision no matter what happens along the way. If I had beat myself up each time I didn't hit a goal right on, I would have quit a long time ago.

As soon as I set out on my current career path, I set a goal for the first year to make a million dollars in personal income. I also set goals to be speaking and teaching seminars all over the country within that year, to have a best-selling book and be the leading authority in my field. None of those things happened. But what did happen was I set myself in a direction that was to become my life's purpose. Although I didn't even come close to my goals that first year, I did make headway. I was teaching seminars in a few different places around the country. I was becoming an expert in my field. Did I beat myself up? No way! I said, "Good job, Chris!" and kept going.

Remember that most people overestimate what they can accomplish in one year's time and underestimate what they can

163

accomplish in a lifetime. This turned out to be very true for me. Within two years of setting my original goals I really was speaking all over the country. Within two and half years I was finally writing my book. Within four years I was speaking internationally. Was this a failure? Not even close. It was a major victory!

Keep your eye on the big picture and your long-term vision, no matter what.

I remember when I was organizing one of my very first seminars years ago I ended up canceling it because I had too few people. A friend of mine said, "Well, you gave the seminar business a shot, what are you going to do now?" Even though I was really upset at the time, I smiled to myself about that kind of thinking. I would never even consider thinking the way he had suggested. Today it's not unusual for our seminars to sell out completely. The people who succeed massively in life realize that there is no such thing as failure. Take everything as feedback because feedback is the breakfast of champions.

TWELVE

Who's on My Team?

"You can have the most beautiful dream in the world,
but it takes people to build it."
~ Walt Disney

You have clarified your vision and how to establish a mission for how you are going to create it. We've discussed how to set up the signposts along the way and the master strategy for success that underpins everything we do. The next step is enrolling others in your vision so you can create leverage and achieve outstanding results. Your team members create the power behind your good ideas that can help you translate your vision into reality. How do you create the fuel that will compel your teammates to drive you powerfully toward your vision? The fuel is created by helping them to achieve their deepest desires—by helping others to self-actualize. By helping enough people to get what they want most, you certainly will get what you want most.

The first thing to do is to think about who you want on your team as you move toward your objectives. Napolean Hill, author of *Think and Grow Rich*, one of the timeless classics in personal development, talks about the mastermind alliance–creating synergy and attracting people to you who will assist in the accomplishment of those goals.

Take a moment now to think of six people, either actual people or roles that you will need to fill in order for you to achieve your goals. Write down the name of a person if you know them and why they are important to the accomplishment of your vision. If you don't know someone specifically, write down the role and why that role is important. You'll be surprised at how quickly the world will conspire toward your success when you get clear about what you need. Next week you might just bump into a person that does exactly what you require.

My Team	How They Will Benefit
1._____	_____
2._____	_____
3._____	_____
4._____	_____
5._____	_____
6._____	_____

Once you've named those people or those roles, make a list of what's going to be their advantages for getting involved in your dream. What's in it for them? How is what you want going to also assist them in attaining what they want? If you don't know the people on your list yet, or if you need a kick start to help you discover how they might be able to benefit through the accomplishment of your vision, you can just imagine yourself floating out of your body and down into their body and imagine you are looking out of their eyes. How could that person benefit from assisting you in your dream?

Once you have begun to identify the major players on your team, your goal then becomes learning how to work best in concert with your team in order to win the Game. This is accomplished first with intention and secondly through communication. The questions you want to constantly be asking yourself are, "How can I assist them to self-actualize through the accomplishment of my vision? How can I help them get what they want most?" Then through your mastery of communication skills, as presented in this third section of *Three Steps to Wealth and Power,* you will be able to maneuver the Playing Field with many players working toward your success!

Of vital importance to you in captivating your team are your sensory acuity and rapport building skills. Master communicators who get others to take action always employ sensory acuity. When pulling together a team, sensory acuity is the act of being aware enough to pick up on the various signals that people give you as you talk to them. Are you really getting through to them or not? This lets you know how to adjust your communication to make sure you are being understood. Have you captured their imagination or not? Are you connecting to this person or not? This is such an important issue for enrolling others into your vision that we will discuss some of the ways you can fine-tune your sensory acuity.

THE IMPORTANCE OF SENSORY ACUITY

"He that has eyes to see and hear may convince himself that no mortal can keep a secret. If his lips are silent, he chatters with his finger tips, betrayal oozes out of him at every pore."
~ Sigmund Freud

Freud here was referring to the fact that we are *always* communicating something, even when we are not using words. People who are outstanding communicators are able to notice things in their sensory awareness that others do not. They are aware of the minutest shifts in the person they are communicating with or even in an audience, and can adjust their communication accordingly to ensure the message is getting through. This is what is called "sensory acuity." To develop your skills and abilities to notice things that most people don't even realize exist will unlock your potential to create the results you desire in your interpersonal communications.

NOTICE MINUTE CHANGES FROM MOMENT TO MOMENT

How would you like a way to know whether your communication is getting through to someone or not? What if you could notice from moment to moment where your communication was going with someone so that you could change it, if necessary, to produce exactly the result that you wanted? Sharpened sensory acuity will allow you to do these things and more.

HALLUCINATION VS. SENSORY FEEDBACK

The most important aspect to remember when beginning to develop your sensory acuity is the difference between sensory feedback and hallucination. Our purpose as we begin to notice the minute changes that happen in those we communicate with from moment to moment is not to guess what they are thinking or what's going on inside of them. Instead, our purpose is to simply realize that something in their physiology, tonality, or energy has changed. These are a few things to look out for:

Pupil Dilation: A person's pupils will range from smaller to larger as they dilate.

Lower Lip Size: The lower lip of an individual will actually change from thinner to fuller. The easiest way to tell the difference is the appearance of lines on the lip when it is full and a stretched smoothness when it is not.

Skin Tone: Skin tone can go from tight to relaxed. This can be noticed by looking at how shiny the skin is, the tighter the skin, the more shine there will typically be.

Skin Color: Skin color can range from lighter to darker, or from pasty to flushed.

Breathing Location: The breathing location of an individual will vary from moment to moment. It can range from high in the chest to low in the belly.

Breathing Rate: Fast or slow.

Muscle Movement: Minute muscle movements can also be noticed and they have the potential of telling us much about the effect of our communication.

You might be wondering at this moment, "Who cares?" The reason these are important is because they indicate a change in state. Calibration is taking one set of distinctions and comparing it to a second set of distinctions. Once you can do this from moment to moment, you can tailor your communication for maximum impact.

For example, I had a client who visited me because he was a procrastinator. He told me how he couldn't get moving and how he just wasn't excited about life anymore. So I talked to him for a while and noticed what he was like when he talked about his life. He was very flat and unenthusiastic. Then I asked him what got him excited in life, what inspired him. He began to talk about his love for waterskiing. The activity itself wasn't as important as the state that he went into when he spoke about it. I noticed that when he started to talk there was a micro muscle movement at the side of his neck, sort of like a twitching. My client was currently taking a lesser non-engaged role in a company he worked in, so I started talking to him about the possibility of becoming a sales manager there, and he wasn't inspired by that. I then used an analogy (very powerful and I'll talk about how to do that in a later chapter) to illustrate my point and see if I could get him to see the possibility. His father had been in the military, so I said, "It's kind of like being the General instead of the foot soldier." We talked about that for a while and because of this analogy he started to see the big picture. As soon as that happened, I noticed this micro muscle movement again. So I was able to monitor whether on not my communication was actually getting through to him because I had developed my sensory acuity skills enough to notice the shifts in calibration.

As well as the micro muscle movement there was also changes in skin color and pupil dilation, which only served to verify his understanding.

By mastering sensory acuity, you become aware of things that most people are not aware of, and that is incredibly useful information in all walks of life, whether in a business negotiation or a romantic relationship. A word of warning however: *avoid attaching meaning to the change.* Sensory acuity is valuable in that you can become aware *of the change* and then you can start to see a correlation between that change and an emotional response. For example, with my procrastinating friend I had no idea what the twitching muscle meant until I had spoken to him for a little while and noticed the correlation between the minute muscle movement and his being excited. That exact same movement may mean something completely different in someone else, so don't start to categorize things as good or bad, just notice the difference and look for connections that can give you a clue to the meaning for that person. Being aware enough and taking the time to be aware enough is a very powerful tool and can assist the deepening of rapport.

THIRTEEN

The Power of Rapport

"Anything is possible in the presence of a good rapport."
~ Milton Erickson

When you look at the most charismatic leaders, there is one fundamental skill that they have—the ability to create instantaneous rapport with anyone. Rapport is a deep and unconscious connection to another person, a feeling that you have a lot in common with them. You are not necessarily getting a person to like you; you are creating an atmosphere where they will recognize that you are alike. This allows them to warm to you, accept and trust you more readily. Good rapport fosters understanding and contrary to popular belief, it is a skill that can be learned. The ability to create rapport is the foundation of great communication and outstanding leadership.

There are two underlying principles of rapport. The first is that when people are similar they tend to like each other. The second is that communication is not just about the words you use.

In 1970, anthropologist Ray L. Birdwhistell, who devoted his entire research career to the study of human communications, wrote the book *Kinesics and Context*. In this book, Dr. Birdwhistell explains that the effect of our communication is less dependent upon words then one might think. In fact, his research revealed that 55% of the effectiveness of any communication is due to the physiology of an individual, whereas 38% is a result of the vocal tonality, and only 7% is a result of the actual words.

PHYSIOLOGY

Physiology is what you are doing with your body. It is the first impression that someone gets and it has an enormous impact on what you are communicating to the world. Your senses are literally being bombarded with information that is being processed so fast you're not even aware of it. This is why physiology is such a huge influence on communication because it occurs before you even open your mouth

What does your physiology say about you? I'm not talking about just your body shape and what you wear. I'm talking about how you hold yourself. Do you look the world straight in the eyes or do you slouch and scuffle around? Do you walk with purpose or amble to your destination? Do you project an air of confidence or trepidation?

How we move is so important to how we feel, and how we feel will very often determine what we do and how people perceive us. There is a set pattern of movement and breathing that is required in order to "do unhappy." Unhappiness is more than just a thought. It is something you communicate to your own body so that it can behave in an unhappy manner.

Anyone can learn how to "do depressed", so why wouldn't you also be able to learn how to "do happiness" or confidence? You can. It's all a matter of communicating those states to your body and having your body respond with the appropriate mannerisms.

TONALITY

Tonality is one of these seemingly innocuous ideas that on the surface doesn't seem to have that much impact. Surely what you say is what you say and that's all there is to it, right? Wrong. Do the following little exercise and you will understand the power of tonality.

Read the first sentence out loud without any emphasis on any word.

"I never said he stole money."

Now read the same sentence out aloud again but put the emphasis on the word underlined.

"I never said he stole money."

"I never said he stole money."

"I never said he stole money."

"I never said he stole money."

"I never said he stole money."

"I never said he stole money."

This is exactly the same sentence, with exactly the same words, in exactly the same word order, yet the meaning implied by the underlined emphasis changes the meaning dramatically each time.

WORDS

Most languages have a fairly huge vocabulary. English, for example, contains 615,000 words. And that's not including technical and scientific terms. That's a tremendous vocabulary. Of those thousands of words, everyone has a slightly different meaning for those words, and things can get a little confusing. Perhaps you have experienced this in your own life where you have said something to someone and they have interpreted it completely differently from what you intended.

Ludwig Witkenstein once said, "All the problems of philosophy are the problems of language." My good friend Alex Docker adds to this, "All the problems of communication are problems of language."

Rapport is the linchpin to successful interpersonal communication and involves using all of the three components of communication—physiology, tonality, and words—to ensure you develop rapport with an individual or group. Rapport enables you to influence people in ways that are positive for them and to create outcomes that are win-wins. At any time in the communication process, if there is a sign of resistance, it may be due to lack of rapport. It becomes a very important skill to learn, because with rapport we can alleviate any resistance to communication.

LIKE ATTRACTS LIKE

The processes of rapport that will be covered in this book are based upon the idea that like attracts like. People who are similar tend to like each other. There is a certain level of comfort in being with people who are similar to you. Haven't you ever had a time when you met someone and you felt as if you had known him or her before? This feeling of connection can also be felt when you meet someone who has experienced something that you have. There is a level of mutual understanding and empathy occuring that instantaneously elevates the conversation to a more familiar and open level.

This feeling of familiarity is often a result of the commonalities you share either at the conscious or subconscious level. Rapport can also be thought of as being a state of trust and responsiveness.

RAPPORT IS NOT LIKING

At any time that I am discussing being "in rapport," I do not necessarily mean liking one another. This is an important distinction. I simply mean communicating in a way that is understood by the other person. And rapport is an essential part of that comprehension equation.

Sometimes it is necessary to communicate with someone in a way that most people would consider dangerous to rapport in order to actually create it. Until his death in 1980, the psychiatrist Dr. Milton Erickson was considered a master of rapport and the world's foremost authority on hypnosis. Dr. Erickson would occasionally come close to what some would call "insulting" his patients and still maintained magnificent rapport.

There is one particular story about Dr. Erickson where he had a client who came to see him because she was overweight. She said she was ashamed because she never had time to spend with her children because she was always too busy. According to the client she was too busy eating and buying candy and cookies. So Dr. Erickson leaned over to the client and said, "You *should* be ashamed. I feel sorry for your poor children growing up in Phoenix, Arizona and never having had the opportunity to visit the Botanical Gardens, or to climb Squaw Peak, or see the Grand Canyon..." He proceeded to list several other of the local outdoor sites and said, "Now go and hang a sign on your bathroom mirror that says '*Let the damn kids grow up in ignorance,*' and you need not look in the mirror, but every time you do, you will be reminded of your kids who will be disenfranchised and grow up not having had the opportunity to see and experience this wonderful place." A year later the woman contacted Dr. Erickson and said, "The kids and I have visited all the sites in and around Phoenix and I've lost twenty pounds. Can I please take that sign off the mirror?!"

If Dr. Erickson had attempted to be nicer in his interaction with the woman or to be liked by her, he might not have achieved the responsiveness that he did by communicating in a manner that got the desired result. His outcome was to help this lady and her outcome was to lose weight. Both goals were achieved because he was able to communicate effectively through establishing the correct rapport.

MATCHING AND MIRRORING PHYSIOLOGY

The process for creating a deep, unconscious rapport is to match and mirror the person you are communicating with. Now for some of you this might sound a bit strange and unusual. The only thing that is strange and unusual about it is that you are bringing into conscious awareness what you have already done unconsciously with those you do have rapport with.

If you ever stop and watch people who are engaged in deep conversation and very responsive to one another, they will be unconsciously matching and mirroring each other. You might find that they are matching and mirroring body posture, head tilt, gestures, volume in speech, or the tempo of their speech. They may be sitting the same way, and if one is leaning forward the other is also leaning forward.

This same type of deep rapport can be created consciously at any time we choose, within a matter of seconds, simply by matching and mirroring the person we are communicating with. Now I have had people take me to task on this and say, "Well Chris, that seems contrived and manipulative." I assure you these skills are about honoring someone's communication style and caring enough about them to communicate in a way that is most acceptable and comfortable to them. The thing about rapport is that when someone else is in rapport with you, then you are also in rapport with him or her. Rapport really offers the potential for making communication a win-win. It's the first step to successful negotiating, which we discuss in more detail later in the book.

For example, have you ever had the experience of talking to someone, where they didn't respond in any way and it felt as if they were very disconnected? It's uncomfortable to be out of rapport with someone. If we can learn skills to stop this from happening consciously then it's a win-win all round.

The process for instantaneous rapport was discovered when researchers Richard Bandler and John Grinder were modeling Dr. Milton Erickson and studying how he was able to create such successful connections with his clients. It was noticed that he would constantly be sitting like his clients and when they would move he would seem to move as well. Erickson was a master of rapport and he placed much emphasis on its use. He was once quoted as saying, "Anything is possible in the presence of a good rapport."

I remember one of the times that I really experienced the powerful effects of using rapport. It was a few years back and I was just starting a business partnership with an acquaintance of mine whom I hadn't seen in years. Interestingly enough, both of us had received extensive training in the techniques of establishing the deep unconscious rapport of which I am describing. When I first sat down to speak with him about our new business venture, immediately I became aware of the fact that we were matching and mirroring each other. Of course, if I hadn't been trained in the technique, I wouldn't have noticed this. At first I asked myself if he was mirroring me consciously, or if was I mirroring him unconsciously? It felt so comfortable, and we were getting along so tremendously, it was as if we were the closest of friends. Soon my conscious awareness of it disappeared completely. The truth was, matching and mirroring as a tool for improved communication had become so second nature to both of us that we did it automatically, without even attempting to do it consciously.

One of my favorite stories of the use of rapport came from one of my clients whom I trained to use rapport to increase his power and influence. He was a politician running for U.S. Senate, and he was used to people recognizing him everywhere and approaching him in a friendly manner. One day he was out getting contributions for his campaign and he stopped by the office of the President of the local Teamsters Union. My politician friend walked into the office accompanied by his campaign manager. The President of the Union was on the telephone and he motioned indignantly for them to sit down. After a while the President hung up the phone, looked at my friend's campaign manager and said in a harsh tone, "Who are you?" The teamster president knew who my friend and his manager were, but he was obviously playing hardball. My friend introduced both himself and his campaign manager. He knew that he was going to have to turn the situation around, as they certainly weren't being warmly welcomed. The teamster said, "You tell me why I should even consider contributing *anything* to your campaign." My friend stood up and walked across the room toward the union leader. He placed his hand on the shoulder of this man and began immediately to match and mirror him. He matched his breathing and his tonality, the phrases he used, and his keywords. He later told me that as soon as he started to do this, the man practically "melted." Not only did he contribute to the campaign but he became a major supporter.

The secret to making the rapport techniques work is to do it just outside of the conscious awareness of the person you are communicating with. This means if you are matching and mirroring gestures the person uses, you wouldn't do them simultaneously with the individual. You wait until it's your turn to speak and then you make similar gestures. This way they become aware of the connection between you on a subconscious level.

REPRESENTATIONAL SYSTEMS

People communicate and internally process information quite differently. By understanding how people process information we can match our communication to their processing style and create an even deeper rapport, once again, at the subconscious level.

We take in information via the five senses: visually, auditorily, kinesthetically, olfactorily, and gustatorily. This can also be described as pictures, sounds, feelings, smells, and tastes. Most people will have what is called a preferred representational system. This is the system that they rely upon predominately to process information. It is important to point out, however, that everyone is using all of the representational systems simultaneously (providing there is no neurological damage or trauma). They will simply have one system that is most familiar to them or comfortable for them to rely upon. People will usually be predominantly visual, auditory, or kinesthetic in their processing and as a result predominantly visual, auditory, or kinesthetic in their communication style.

There is a fourth category as well, which is known as auditory digital. Auditory digital simply means the self-talk we have inside of our heads. There is a whole category of people that prefer to process things through their internal dialogue. It is quite easy to notice someone's preferred representational system once you know what to look out for.

VISUAL REPRESENTATIONAL SYSTEM

People who are predominantly visual tend to speak at a fairly fast rate. These are people who process in pictures. You've heard before that "a picture paints a thousand words." So people who process visually will process faster than they can actually verbalize. This is why they speak so quickly. They will tend to breathe high in the chest. They move from place to place rather quickly and may have difficulty just sitting around. The visual processor will also tend to use visual predicates in their speech. Predicates are simply words that we use to describe our experiences. They may say things like, "Do you see what I mean?" or "I get the picture," or "I've got this thing mapped out clearly."

When making a purchase, a visual processor will be interested in the "look" of something. They will need to "see what you're talking about" before investing. In making a decision, it will have to "appear to be" the right course of action. The visual person learns best by seeing things or by watching demonstrations. Using slides, flipcharts, and diagrams are their methods of instruction.

179

In communicating your vision to someone who is a visual processor, you can also match your communication to their preference and thereby create a deeper interest on their part. Match the predicates that they use and speak in visual terms. To teach them or give them instructions, "show" a visual person exactly how to do what it is that they are learning. Use charts, graphs, and other types of visual aids. In speeches and presentations, paint vivid pictures and description through your language to make things clear and compelling for them. Whether you are one-on-one or in front of a group, you can mirror their large gestures and check in with them from time to time by saying, "Do you see what I mean?" Or "You get the picture, right?"

Approximately 40% of the population is visual.

AUDITORY REPRESENTATIONAL SYSTEM

Next, are the auditory processors. Roughly 20% of the population has either auditory tonal or auditory digital preferences. Someone who is primarily auditory will be most interested in how things sound to them. They will be very aware of the tonality of your voice. Often an auditory person's vocal qualities will be well modulated and they might even sound like a television presenter or a radio announcer. The language they use to describe their experience will be with words like, "that sounds good," or "that rings a bell," or "you're coming through loud and clear." Let their language guide you to the most effective way to speak to them where they're at.

When making a purchase, the auditory person will be most interested in whether or not it "sounds" like a good purchase. In making decisions, it will need to "sound" like the right thing to do. In learning something new, the sound effects used will be quite important for them to connect with and recall it later. The auditory preference is split in that there are people who process primarily auditorily (or auditory tonal) and auditory digital (or self-talk). In order to make distinctions between the two, auditory digital will be discussed as an entirely different category.

Auditory Tonal

With the auditory tonal person we can create a deeper rapport and understanding by matching their predicates, saying things like "How does that sound?" or "Does that resonate well with you?" We can facilitate their learning most effectively by speaking in pleasant tones and using a lot of vocal variation to hold their attention. They will be very sensitive to the tonality of voice of those they communicate with.

Auditory Digital

These are people who tend to process things primarily through the secondary experience of internal dialogue, "digital" simply referring to the individual words they use internally. They have a high need to talk to themselves about their subjective experience and make sense of it all, because it is the "logical thing to do." People who are primarily auditory digital processors will be interested in logic and reason. In making decisions, the choice must always make sense. Often, even in things such as romantic relationships, they have reasonable criteria for their decisions. They will choose to be with someone because it makes sense. The pros will outweigh the cons.

In making purchases, the auditory digital processor will most likely be interested in analyzing or going over all of the features of what it is that they are considering purchasing to make sure that it meets all of their criteria for making a logical decision.

When teaching or speaking to a person who processes highly in the auditory digital representational system, it will be important to give them lots of facts and figures as they are interested in research and data to prove things that have been said are true.

The auditory digital person may sometimes seem slightly

dissociated or removed when you are communicating with them. You can create deeper levels of rapport with the auditory digital processors by mirroring any dissociation. You can assist them in making a decision by showing logical reasons for action. You can also increase their understanding of a certain subject or topic by matching this processing style.

KINESTHETIC REPRESENTATIONAL SYSTEM

People who are primarily kinesthetic processors will tend to speak very slowly and deliberately. They may go inside and check their feelings about what they are going to say before actually verbalizing it. Kinesthetic processors will talk about their feelings and the predicates they use will involve touch and feeling. They'll say things like, "I don't feel right about that," "I really need to get a grasp on that concept," or "I want to get in touch with her."

When making a purchase, the kinesthetic processor will need to "feel good about it." They would certainly need to try clothes on before they bought them to make sure they "feel right." In teaching a kinesthetic processor, it's important to include exercises so that they can actually "do" what it is that is being taught and get "a feel for it." People who are kinesthetic will often make decisions based on their gut instinct.

We can create deeper rapport with someone who is kinesthetic by matching their breathing, which is generally low in the belly; by slowing down; by using kinesthetic predicates to describe experience; and by avoiding large, exaggerated gestures or lists of reasons. Roughly 40% of the population is primarily kinesthetic processors.

MATCHING AND MIRRORING VOICE

There are several components of the voice we can mirror. The primary components are the tone, tempo, timbre, and volume. However, the easiest ways to match and mirror voice is to stick to tempo and volume. It is quite easy to match the speed someone is speaking with and as well as their volume, without looking as though you're mimicking them.

Remember that matching works best outside of conscious awareness, so it needs to be subtle. Mirroring a voice can be particularly powerful on the phone.

KEYWORDS

Other things that can be matched include keywords or phrases that the person uses. Keywords can be any words that you hear the person say unusually often.

These can be very useful in selling. Whether you are selling products, services, or ideas they can assist you in the communication process. One of the most important things a salesperson can do is to LISTEN! The client *will* tell you how to best communicate your offer for maximum success. Use your sensory acuity to be aware when they are conveying their needs directly or indirectly.

Everyone has a particular way of expressing themselves. If you pay attention to the subtlety of their language you can mirror phrases they use back to them. This has the effect of making an unconscious connection and the other person feels comfortable and understood.

You will know when someone is in rapport with you just by how the conversation is progressing. It feels very easy and comfortable. Another great clue is pacing and leading. This is when you change your physiology in some way and the person you are communicating with unconsciously follows you. For example, you might be sitting with your legs crossed and as you uncross them the person you are communicating with will uncross their legs simultaneously or within a few moments thereafter.

BREAKING RAPPORT

Sometimes it is highly appropriate to break rapport. There are some people who you may choose not to be in rapport with. There are some people in the world who do not have your highest intention in mind, and it may not be appropriate to ever enter into rapport with them. Also, if someone is not respecting your personal boundaries either knowingly or unknowingly, it may be necessary to break rapport. The process is easy to do. It's as simple as breaking eye contact and turning away. A good and effective way to break rapport is to do it with no negativity toward the other person. Simply move away from them. This will cause less ill-will between you and allow you to preserve your boundaries.

Always remember that rapport opens the gateway to communication. It's a powerful way of opening up dialogue so that you can then create synergistic relationships. Rapport building techniques are not a means to an end. They are the beginning of a process that is developed and nurtured through trust and helping others get what they want. This ultimately leads to getting what you want.

FOURTEEN

Values – The Key to Influence and Inspiration

"I consider my ability to arouse enthusiasm among men the greatest asset I possess."
~ Charles Schwab

Master communicators throughout history all seem to have an innate gift of knowing what others need and want, and finding a way of delivering that within the bigger context of what they also want. Mobilizing, motivating, and inspiring others are skills that some say you are just born with. I disagree. Anyone can develop leadership skills if you pay attention to people's needs and understand their values.

Values are simply what is important to people. We have talked about them earlier in the context of working out your own values and how they impact on your reality. Here we will be looking at them in terms of how to recognize and understand other people's values. By doing so you can enroll them into your vision and gain leverage in a way that ensures they get what they want while moving your vision forward too. Because we all have a different model of the world, it is valuable to be able to recognize key indicators of that model, and therefore what motivates someone, you then have the opportunity to explain your vision, a proposal, or sale in the language that the other person totally relates to. This increases the chances of synergy and involvement considerably.

EVOLUTION OF VALUES

The Model of Values below comes from Dr. Clare Graves, a former professor at Union University. What's interesting about this work is that, rather than being based on hypothesis, it is the result of detailed research on people and history.

According to Graves, individuals, societies, and cultures have an evolution of Values Systems, or ways of thinking about and perceiving their world that tend toward certain behavior patterns. They then cycle through each progressive value level as a reaction to the inadequacies of the previous level. Each value level is a response to the previous one in an upward spiral. It has been said that the solutions of today are the problems of tomorrow and that's how it is with this values spiral. Each value level has its own issues inherent with it. Therefore, each new level upwards must adapt the thinking of the previous level to address the new wave of issues that arise.

An understanding and awareness of these different levels of thought that people operate from will increase your communication mastery, and therefore your ability to produce results a thousandfold, with and through others. Truly learning this information alone will make you an extraordinary communicator. I will give you an overview of Values levels first as evolving global thought systems then discuss in more depth how they are manifested on an individual basis and how you can apply it to improve your daily communication. The eight Values levels are described by Dr. Clare Graves as follows:

Values Level 1
Survival

> This level doesn't really exist in society today, other than in newborn babies, but was prevalent in early times before people banded together in tribes. It is very instinctive and is the basic drive to survive. A child, when he

or she is born, is only interested in eating and sleeping and doing what it needs to do to survive. As humans developed, however, they realized it was just too hard to survive on their own so they started to band together to form tribes.

Values Level 2
Tribal

This values level was reached when people started to come together to form tribes because it was the best form of protection. It's a subservient level where there was an expectation of sacrifice for the chief. As evolution has taken place, however, ego has emerged more strongly and the drive for power has overridden the sacrifice mentality as new potential chiefs vie for power.

Values Level 3
Aggression and Power

This is the values level of might is right, where the strong dominate the weak, and rebellion is the order of the day. What happens in this level is that the young challenge the old. Over time there is a realization that this can't continue, so a desire for systems and stability emerges.

Values Level 4
Systems

This is the value level that says there is one best way, that system and order are good. Obedience and discipline have overtaken from the last level of risk, aggression, and disorder. Here we earn reward by hard work and order. Authority is king and we seek to belong to a system and find comfort from being part of the collective. This is the home of rigid thinking and many of the "isms" belong here—Communism, Catholicism, terrorism, etc. Most of the world religions fall into values level four thinking, which is, "sacrifice now for reward later."

The urge to break free from that rigidity by rebelling once again shows up and there is a move to break out and seek reward, which then leads to...

Values Level 5
Success

This is the level most concerned with achievement. The mottos of the success oriented might be, "make it happen!" "Just do it!" It's the level where the world is a marketplace for entrepreneurs to profit. The level is often materialistic, although the motivation is often more about the sense of achievement that comes from the accumulation of material wealth rather than the material wealth itself. The evolution of this level is that people get to a later stage in life and realize that all that accumulation hasn't made them happy or complete, and they feel a "hole in their soul." This is often when they move onto...

Values Level 6
Group and Cause-oriented

This is where people turn inward instead of outward for fulfillment and happiness. Happiness is not dependant on the number of toys or material possessions but rather on a sense of contribution and community. The drawback of level 6 thinking is that it can become too democratic. When everyone is equal and has a right to their opinion as truth, sometimes in the quest for consensus, nothing actually gets done. This can also be the most controlling values level because it may preach love and acceptance of everybody but only if you also love and accept everybody. This causes frustration again due to the lack of tangible results. It may feel good but there is inevitably a move to make things happen more effectively and people move to the next level.

Values Level 7
Functional Flow

The drive for individuality pushes through and breaks out the mold of acceptance. There is an understanding of the paradoxical nature of the world. To experience life you must experience all of life, not just the pockets of acceptable behavior. People who function on this level will not turn their backs on the causes and the ideals of level 6, but will instead be focused on living those ideals, while also breaking away from the group and exploring all that life has to offer. Level 7 people are constantly learning. They will listen and take in a great deal of differing views. They will take on what they choose and what feels right for them at that time but are not set in their views. They are flexible in their thinking and are not overly attached to anything, be it ideas, beliefs, or physical possessions. Values level 7 is the first values level that is able to move throughout all the previous levels with volition depending upon what works best at the time.

The downside to level 7 is that sooner or later the exploring lone wolf gets bored and as they may not have any concrete goals, once again begins moving onto the next level searching for something more meaningful.

Values Level 8
The planet does matter

Values level 8 begins to look at the world in a new way. They see the world as being one living entity with themselves being a microcosm of the macrocosm. They are most interested in who they become as a result of how they relate to the whole.

The reason these are so important to you is because truly understanding the values levels allows you to tailor your communication to every individual on your team with their values level so that your vision relates to them in the most compelling way to them. First, this creates an even greater level of rapport. Second, you have linked your communication to their greatest motivations.

When you can determine someone's thinking resides mostly in values level 5, you can construct your proposal to that person very differently than the proposal to a level 6 person, emphasizing those things that fulfill their level 5 motivations. Say for example you had written a book and you were sitting down to propose it to a publisher. If that publisher had earlier mentioned how hard they had worked to get where they are and that they were looking to become Senior Editor, because the prestige and notoriety was important to them, their thinking is likely centered at values level 5, perhaps even with some level 4 demonstrated by their loyalty to the company. By listening to their communication about what was important to them, you may say, "My last book sold 500,000 copies worldwide which generated $6 million. This new one I just wrote is likely to do the same if not better."

If your publisher had spent more of your conversation talking about how much she loves her job because of all the people they help with their books and the impact she was making on the conscious-minded community, she would be demonstrating more level 6 thinking. Then your previous pitch wouldn't be nearly as effective because money and status may not be as high on her list of values. Instead you could say, "I have written a new book. As you know, I am dedicated to the expansion of human consciousness and providing information and tools so that everyone can find their place in the world and find happiness and fulfillment." Sure, you would also add the dollars but it is not the dollars that will inspire a level 6 person. Remember that you should only say things if they are actually true, but if you are communicating with someone of a specific values level you can simply "tailor" your communication to fit their model of the world.

When you are aware of someone's value level, you can speak their language to get them inspired and involved in your vision while also feeling as though they are also furthering their cause and what is important to them. This is a perfect win-win. (As long as what you say is also true. Remember to keep your communication "ecological" in that your objectives are safe for everyone.)

RECOGNIZING VALUES THROUGH BEHAVIOR

Remember that these aren't types of people but rather systems of thought inside people. These categories aren't intended to pigeonhole people, rather to serve as useful information when communicating with them. Also remember that someone may be a combination of different levels in different areas of their life. They may demonstrate, for example, level 5 thinking in business and 3 in relationships.

To assist you in recognizing the different levels, here are some more things to watch out for when figuring out what is important to the people with whom you're dealing.

The odd number values levels 1, 3, 5, 7 are focused on self, whereas the even number value levels 2, 4, 6, 8 are focused on others and sacrificing for others.

The odd and even values levels also see their locus of control as coming from different areas. The odd values levels see their locus of control as being internal. In other words, they perceive themselves as being in control of their own destiny. The even values levels believe that the locus of control is external. It's about the external world and how they relate to it as part of a community.

Interestingly enough, however, the focus is different also. While the odd numbers think of themselves as being in control, focus is on the external world to create it the way they want. So they use that internal power to design the external world around them.

With the sacrificial levels 2, 4, 6 and 8 their locus of control is external yet their focus is internal. They are more interested in working out who they become as a result of what they are doing with the group or the cause; how they feel about themselves as a result of doing what they do.

Values Level 1 – exist as part of nature, acting more instinctively much like other animals.

Values Level 2 – show tribal tendencies, banding together for safety to placate spirits and nature. Their ritualistic behaviors are motivated by their sense that the external world is full of mystery and danger beyond their ability to control.

Values Level 3 – think "it's a jungle out there." Their behavior shows their belief in the survival of the fittest, where each must fend for him or herself, control or be controlled.

Values Level 4 – are strongly influenced by a need for structure and the belief that the world is controlled by a higher power, whether that represents a divine entity, the church, or the company they work for, for fifty years. They are motivated by doing the "right" thing, therefore they tend to be driven by a sense of guilt. If they are not doing the "right" thing, they believe they should feel guilty or be punished accordingly. This belief would obviously govern someone's behavior. As a result they will obey, often without question, whomever they believe to be the rightful authority.

Values Level 5 – see the world as full of opportunities for materialistic gain. Therefore, they can tend to be opportunistic or "go-getters", relating everything to money and how it could serve them on their drive to succeed. Level 5 behaviors might be motivated by that old '80's motto, "He who dies with the most toys wins." They also like to be in control because they know best what's "right" for them personally. Therefore, they operate best with autonomy and authority, such as running their own businesses.

Value Level 6 – live life with wider social concerns, feel themselves to be part of a larger connected humanity. Personal growth and a shared sense of community are important to them. They feel good when they are contributing to society.

Values Level 7 – perceives the world around them as a complex system at risk of collapse. They are primarily motivated by learning, being free, and questioning things as they are. They change and explore the world as it serves their interests at the time.

Values Level 8 – seeks balance and order beneath the Earth's chaos. These seemingly rare individuals maintain a global perspective in all of their actions because they are aware of the interdependence of every living thing.

RECOGNIZING VALUES THROUGH DECISION-MAKING CRITERIA

The following is the criteria that each level would typically use when making decisions. What types of activities people choose to be involved in or which proposals to accept, even what cars to buy, are determined by what is important to them—their primary values. These responses show what each level would consider when choosing if something is a "good idea" or the "right" thing for them to do. As you read this, be thinking about how you can apply all this information to better understand your own values as well as how to choose others to assist you in reaching your goals.

Level 2 – Because the "tribe" or social group is central to their existence, Level 2 will decide to do something based on whether their leader or chieftan approves.

Level 3 – Because immediate rewards are paramount to a Level 3 and they tend to act impulsively, they will choose what's best to do by saying, "Let's do it! It will get me what I want right now!" They might also decide between options based on outsmarting someone else or beating them to the punch, be it a dog-eat-dog world. By the way, you can't get a Level 3 to rise to action using guilt, as you could a Level 4—Level 3 thinkers just don't feel guilt, although they can feel shame.

Level 4 – Since Level 4s like to follow the rules to avoid punishment and be loyal to their duty, they make a choice by saying, "That's the right thing to do because it's in line with the establishment." Or in line with company policy, is what is expected of me by my family or follows the law to the letter. Remember that they will be looking to comply with their own outside authority.

Level 5 – They will be looking to determine which option furthers their own ambitions or material gain. If it assists them on their way they will bend the rules and their values to any situation to win. This is called situational ethics. Level 5 chooses what's best for achieving their objectives saying, "I'm going to go for it because it is to my greater advantage."

Level 6 – Having a bigger picture in mind that includes everyone, Level 6 will try to make decisions by consensus.

They choose what to do by saying, "That's a good idea because everyone agrees."

Level 7 – Level 7 will tend to make decision based upon how they know and feel within themselves, regardless of what others think. They take responsibility for their actions and make sure what they do is ecological, while still being egocentric. A Level 7 will choose what to do by saying, "That will work best because it functions well personally and on every level."

Level 8 – They believe that collective individualism serves the entire living system best, so would take the Earth into consideration when making any decisions. They seek ways to benefit the living system they are an integral part of. Level 8 will choose what to do by saying, "That's the right thing to do because it fits with nature's patterns and will benefit the whole."

VALUES IN SELF-PERCEPTION AND RELATIONSHIPS

It's important not to judge the values levels. One is not better than the other. It's not a competition to "get to the top." Some people will move through the values levels during the course of their life and others will not. They are important only when you start to recognize the levels in people around you through the language they use and the behaviors and decision-making criteria they employ. You can also pick up on an individual's values level by his or her apparent self-perception and relationships to others.

Sometimes values level 6 people would like to think of themselves as 8s. The 5s want to be the best, so whatever that is they want to be it! A 3 will look at everyone else as suckers. The 4 will see everyone as wrong and will often mistake a 7 or a 5 and think they are a 3. The 5 will look at an 8 as a 6 and sometimes at a 7 and see a 3.

There are also some insidious relationships that develop between the levels. For example a 6 may be in relationship with a 3 because they think they can save them. The 3 will like that relationship because they will think they can use the 6. The 5 will often get into a relationship with a 2 because the 2 will stay home and mind the family while the 5 goes out and creates. The 7 will stay in a relationship as long as it serves them and then they are off to the next, not in a callous way but often because they've learned from that relationship and are moving on.

By truly understanding the value levels, you will master a whole new level of communication. You will be able to literally make your communication most compelling regardless of the content of communication. This information is especially powerful if you can combine the values level with the more specific values of the individual. This can be done through either direct elicitation or indirect elicitation.

ELICITING VALUES

If you are going to do a direct elicitation, it may be necessary to tell your client, prospect, or team member what you are about to do. This is also known as a pre-frame. When I am doing formal values elicitation with a client, I will sometimes say, "To save you time and best serve you, would it be O.K. if I asked you a few questions?"

Then simply ask the question, "What's important to you in a business relationship?" When you are coming from a good place, your understanding of the client's values will really assist you in creating a long-term working relationship.

You can also do formal values elicitations around the product or service they are buying. A good example of this is a realtor representing a buyer who's looking for a new house. The question is, "What's important to you in a house?" Outstanding realtors know exactly what their buyers want.

This is also a great process when going for interviews or pitching for new business. I remember asking a prospective boss, "What's important to you in someone who works for you?" The moment I asked that question, many things were revealed to me. He gave me a list of the following valued qualities:

- Team player
- Learning and Growing
- Enthusiastic
- Hard working

This was extremely important information for me. Once I knew exactly what he wanted in an employee, I could then give examples of my past experience that demonstrated those values. Needless to say, I got the job and it also gave me incredible peace of mind while I was working there. I never had to worry or wonder about what he thought of my work. I knew exactly what to do to satisfy him. He was thrilled with my job performance and I was content and at ease knowing that I was doing the right things. I effectively sold myself to the company on a daily basis through the fulfillment of my employer's values.

FIFTEEN

Powerful Sales and Negotiation

"It is one of the most beautiful compensations of this life that no man can sincerely try to help another without helping himself."

~ Ralph Waldo Emerson

In his book *40 Day Mind Fast Soul Feast*, Dr. Reverend Michael Beckwith tells us that in order to live the life we are meant to live we must, "Stop working, start serving!" What he means is that the moment we come from an intention of serving others, we make our own lives more fulfilling and create the opportunity to increase our own personal prosperity. He goes on to explain, "Ralph Waldo Emerson said that we place the Universe in our debt as we give more than we are compensated for, if we don't work for mere money alone. Since we cannot out-give the self-givingness of the spirit, the Universe will create opportunities to give even more back to us than we could ever give to it."

A lot of people go through life looking for what they can "get out of it." It is the least effective way of approaching things. If you are unsatisfied, it is nothing but a reflection of the value, or worth, you are adding. Instead of asking, "What can I get?" ask, "What can I give?" I guarantee you your fortune will change... almost overnight.

When you go into a situation to see what you can give and you create value for others, you are compensated for it with

199

money, which is our means of measuring and exchanging value. If you create tremendous value for others and you do it intelligently, you will get tremendous financial rewards. This is the basis of the law of reciprocity.

Dr. Genie Laborde, in the book *Influencing With Integrity*, speaks of the process of dovetailing outcomes. This means making certain that every communication outcome you have is win-win, where both parties profit. This, I believe, is one of the most important aspects of most interpersonal interactions. When your outcomes are not win-win, you will earn a reputation as being someone who is self-serving and you may fool some people for a while but your long-term success will be adversely affected. When your outcomes are win-win and "dove-tailed," you foster good will amongst the people you deal with. You, as well as those you are involved with, will prosper, and you will earn a reputation that brings you much success.

A few years back I was speaking at a business camp with Brian Tracy who is known as one of America's leading sales authorities. One evening as I was having dinner with Brian, I asked him what advice he would give to someone who was just starting in business, and he said, "Never forget to sell yourself. Nobody else will do it for you. You've always got to be selling yourself."

- What makes a winning politician? Their ability to sell themselves to their constituents.
- What makes a winning trial attorney? Their ability to sell their client's case and effectively win over the judge and jury.
- What makes an effective communicator of any type? Their ability to sell their ideas and concepts to others.
- What makes an effective parent? Their ability to sell their values and behavioral boundaries better than those who might influence their child negatively.

Gandhi was a very intelligent lawyer skilled in persuasive communication before turning to champion the freedom of his people. He knew how to sell his ideas. This allowed him to be amazingly effective at negotiating with the British who were in power at the time. He was equally effective with his ability to sell his ideas of non-violence to the world. So sales and negotiating are not too different a process—within selling is often some negotiating. And successful negotiations always require a little selling. It's all about finding out what both sides need then filling those needs. In this chapter, you will learn the specific steps to both selling and negotiating.

THE WIN-WIN SELLING PROCESS

> *"We are all salesmen every day of our lives. We are selling our ideas, our plans, our enthusiasms to those with whom we come in contact."*
>
> ~ Charles Schwab

One of the greatest gifts we have as human beings is imagination. Selling is all about leading the imagination of the client to a place where they can really connect with and become inspired by the experience of having your product, service, or idea. Great visionaries and leaders in history often seem to innately possess this ability, but it can also be learned.

Learning to powerfully sell your ideas is essential to your success in any field. The following is a precise, easy to remember selling process that will allow you to lead someone's imagination in such a way that compels them to take the actions you suggest. To make it easier to recall the steps in any situation, just think of the acronym:

S.O.A.R. TO R.I.C.H.E.S

S.O.A.R. represents the all-important phase of interviewing your prospect. It stands for:

S. Situation

   Find out about their current situation

O. Objectives

   Find out what the client wants right now

A. Antecedents

   Find out whatever stands in their way of having what they want

R. Rewards

   Find out what rewards the client will get as a result of getting what they want

R.I.C.H.E.S. represents all the things that need to take place for there to be a buying commitment:

R. Rapport

I. Interview

C. Course of Action

H. How would you like to pay for that?

E. Excite the client

S. Serve and Satisfy

Remember that we are always selling something. So when I use the terms "prospect" or "client," keep in mind how this process serves *your* goals specifically. A prospect could be an individual you are considering hiring for your team, a company you are making a proposal to or even someone you want to come away with you for the weekend, in which case the step "how would you like to pay for that?" may not apply (although you never know!). In any case, utilize all you can. It works. I know from experience. It is one of the fastest and most effective ways to get to a win-win buying commitment.

First, I will cover the specific information you need to obtain during the interview process. Then you will understand what I am referring to in the steps to R.I.C.H.E.S.

INTERVIEW QUESTIONING FLOW

Asking questions is one of the most important aspects of win-win selling because you discover what is most important to your prospect, which tells you what will compel them toward taking action. Once you've established rapport, the interview phase gets you to better understand the client's needs and values. That's why it is sometimes termed "gap analysis"—discovering where the client is now, where they want to be, and whether or not your product, service, or idea can bridge the gap.

My good friend Joe Hasson of Thomas Kiblen and Associates calls this questioning stage the "heart of the sale." He uses the analogy of an artichoke. What is the best part of an artichoke? The heart is. To get to the heart you've got to peel away the leaves and scoop out the gunk on top. That's the questioning process. S.O.A.R questioning is extremely effective. Here's how you do it:

S. Situational Questions

Situational questions allow us to understand the current situation of a prospect, prospective client, or employer. They tell us about the company or the individual. This also assists us in deepening rapport and building credibility because it shows that we are genuinely interested in this person or group. In selling sales trainings, for example, we would ask the following types of situational questions:

- How many people do you have in your company?
- How long have you been working here?
- How did you choose to get into this line of work?
- How many sales are you making on a monthly basis?

Think for a moment about what it is you are selling. Are you selling your products or services? Are you selling yourself for a promotion or a raise? What is it that you sell? If your answer is "nothing," think again. If you *were* selling something, what would it be?

Situation questions give their current situation. A good thing to do is write your own list of situation questions and memorize them so that you don't have to consciously come up with questions during the interview. You can instead fully focus and stay present with your prospect creating a deeper rapport.

Write down six situation questions that you could ask someone with whom you may find yourself in a selling situation in the near future:

1._____

2._____

3._____

4._____

5._____

6._____

O. Objective Questions

Objective questions allow us to better understand what the other party wants to achieve in their life or their business. The presupposition inherent in asking the questions, "What should you be doing?" or "What do you want to be doing instead?" is that they are not currently doing it. This will tell you what the client or prospect would like to happen instead, what are their ultimate goals that you will be able to assist them with.

Again, using the scenario of selling a sales training or going into a company as a business consultant, here are some sample questions you can ask to reveal their objectives:

- What should you be doing?
- How much business is your top salesperson doing?

- How do you rate in comparison with your competition?
- What are your current goals?
- How close are you to your current goals?
- What expectations do you have on yourself or your department?

Once again, take a few moments now to write down six objective questions to ask the same person you were thinking about in the previous exercise:

1. _____

2. _____

3. _____

4. _____

5. _____

6. _____

A. Antecedent Questions

It's time to ask the antecedent, or "barrier" questions. These questions give the consultative salesperson the important information of what is preventing the client, prospect, or individual from accomplishing their goals. Much in the same way that a therapist probes for what is causing problems, a consultative salesperson looks for their barriers to success. Examples of questions that reveal this type of information are as follows:

- What is preventing you from having what you want in your business or life?
- What has stopped you from creating the type of results that you want?
- What's stopped you from training your other salespeople to produce as much as your top salesperson?
- What is getting in your way?

Take a moment now to write six antecedents type questions:

1. _____

2. _____

3. _____

4. _____

5. _____

6. _____

R. Reward Questions

Finally, we are left with reward questions. These questions supply us with what will be the positive "toward" motivation for taking action and influencing behavior. What specific benefits will the person get by resolving their barriers and producing their ideal objectives? What will their end result be? And what will they potentially miss out on if they don't take action? An easy question to ask is, "When you have ___(*goals*)___, what will that get for you or allow you to do?" This question will give you the reward for the individual with whom you're working. You are now tapping into their dream or vision.

Quite often, their first response to a reward question will not be enough information for the effective consultative salesperson. It's necessary to find out more. The way to do this is to tap into their values. You ask them, "What's important to you about that?" When they give you the initial reward answer, you say, "What's important to you about that?" Then ask them, "When you have (their value) what will you be doing?" This will provide valuable information to be used later in the selling process. The idea behind these final questions is to ascertain their values around the situation and specifically, how the solution could tap into their values.

Take a moment now to write six reward type questions for your prospect:

1._____
2._____
3._____
4._____
5._____
6._____

If you can engage the imagination of your prospect using the S.O.A.R questioning technique, your chances of success are greatly improved. Now that you understand what I mean when I say "interview," let's start at the beginning with:

R. Rapport

The first step in the win-win selling process is to develop rapport. However, rapport should be established and maintained throughout your whole encounter because the essence of rapport is having that person stay responsive to you. There are countless ways to do that. People stay connected with you when they know you sincerely care about their needs. You're not just making a sale; you are making a friend. So ask yourself how would you be with a friend? You talk about your mutual interests, inquire about their needs and desires, share stories... you might even give a friend a gift. And one of the best gifts you can give to someone, one that means the most, is to listen to them. Don't underestimate how great you make someone feel by just listening. Consider what makes you feel connected to someone else, and then offer the same. Know that people will sense if you are not sincere.

I. Interview

Questions are the only way to sell. This is where the art of really listening is so vital. The effective salesperson is not the person who talks people into things they don't need or want. An effective salesperson is a matchmaker between a product, service, or idea and the people that need or want them. To presume that you know what everyone needs without knowing anything about them is to close the doors to the magic that makes true sales professionals successful.

One of the most important aspects of modern selling is to use a consultative approach, not closing sales but instead opening relationships. An outstanding salesperson becomes a highly valued consultant to the person or group they are working with. The best consultants are explorers and discoverers. They uncover where they can be of assistance and assist the prospect to make the connections that cause them to want to buy. The first step is to uncover vital information about their values and desires. This is where the S.O.A.R. criteria for interviewing comes in. Much in the same way that an archaeologist digs for hidden treasures that lay buried beneath the surface, the salesperson can excavate what a client truly wants and needs through questioning what there situation is, their objectives, any barriers, and the rewards they are ultimately seeking.

Then there is something called test close questions that gauge the prospect's temperature and tell you where they are in the sales process. As you begin to connect your product with their true motivations and desires, you can check in with them to make sure you're both still in agreement with questions as simple as, "how does that sound to you so far?" If they are answering "yes" with each test close, and showing other buying signals such as leaning forward, or smiling enthusiastically or even reaching for their wallet, you are moving inevitably forward toward your sale. Because you are addressing all their objections along the way, you will not be hit with them at the end as you are pulling out your pen. Sometimes it will be clear to you by paying attention to your prospect's buying signals that they are ready to move forward right away. If that's the case, skip the chase. Show them the dotted line.

Even knowing what they *don't* want will serve you in knowing what they are motivated to move *away* from. Surprisingly, people react much quicker to avoid pain than to move toward something they want. We all take much quicker action to pull our hand away from a hot stove than we will reaching for the refrigerator. An amazing amount of people live in denial of their real issues, in terms of what the problem is and why they aren't getting what they want in their career or their lives. We do them a great disservice if we don't get them to see what's not working and get them to access their discomfort or discontent about it. It is often the negative feelings that finally motivate people to take constructive action. This means, in order to gain true leverage, you can get your prospect to associate or link in their own mind not having your product with experiencing discomfort. If toward-motivation isn't compelling enough for them to see your vision, away-from motivation can move them to respond faster. No one wants to get burned. All of this can be done through questioning during the interview process.

C. Course of Action

From the interview, we have ascertained whether they have a need or want that we can solve. If they don't, we thank them and leave. If they do, we get them to see how we can help them fulfill their goals. Since you have taken the necessary time to listen and ascertain what is most important to them, you have done enough trial closes along the way to address any objections or concerns on their part, and you are in a position to close the deal with certainty that you can serve and satisfy them. The next step is to use the power of assumption and simply lay out the best course of action by saying, "Here's how we're going to solve your problem," or "get you what you want." Then add your description of how they can use your product, service, or idea. You are now showing them exactly how they can fulfill the desires you uncovered earlier. This basically serves as the final close because you've already answered their concerns throughout the interview. The rest is just working out the details.

H. How would you like to pay for it?

If you've done your job correctly upfront—gained rapport, asked questions, provided the right solutions—gaining buying commitment is as simple as asking "how do you want to pay for it?" A lot of people put too much emphasis on closing. Closing the sale just means asking for the order. When you go to K-Mart and go up to the check-out counter with your purchases, the cashier doesn't get all weird when they ask, "how do you want to pay for it?" Frankly, closing is the easiest part.

E. Excite Your Client

You always want to excite your client about not just your product or proposal, but the benefits of how it will serve their desires. I specify their wants over their needs because it is their deepest wants that truly motivate people toward action. Your own conviction and enthusiasm about your product will transfer from you to them. Transfer your own excitement to them then have them associate, link in their mind, your product with what would give them the most pleasure.

This can be done in a couple of different ways. One is through exciting them with end-result imagery. You used your own end-result imagery when you set your goals in the C.R.E.A.T.E. format. End-result imagery becomes equally effective when applied to the process of selling. It represents what they want to receive, including the positive emotional state, from your product. It is the process of assisting the buyer to access their imagination to create a visual image and corresponding positive emotional state of how your product, service, or idea will enrich their life.

So for example, if your prospect said that the ultimate benefit from having their challenges solved is that they would be able to spend time with their family in Milan, Italy, then at the appropriate moment in the sales process you could say, "Picture this, it's six months from now and you and your family are in Milan enjoying yourselves and you feel so good when you think to yourself, 'I'm sure glad I took that sales training, because that's what's allowed me to create this.' That's what you want, right?" Even a question like, "Wouldn't that be great?" gets them saying yes. Once they have agreed with you enough times, any objections they had suddenly don't weigh in as much as do their desires.

That visual fantasy can be given additional impact by working in all of the representational systems–pictures, sounds, feelings, tastes, smells, and self-talk. Exciting your client can actually be used throughout the win-win selling process wherever you deem appropriate. The full sensory experience that you create in their mind through using end-result imagery will be based on information that you have elicited in the questioning phase of the sale.

S. Serve and Satisfy the Client

The final step of the win-win selling process is not really an ending but a beginning. It's the beginning of a long-term relationship. This step is all about serving and satisfying your client. It's been said that if you help enough people get what they want surely you will get what you want.

A good example of this win-win selling process in action

was when I was negotiating for a job with a training organization. Watch how, although I was in "negotiations", I used the win-win selling process to serve everyone well. I was negotiating back and forth with the vice president of the company, and we were hung up on the amount of money that I was to be paid if I accepted the job. At one point, through my interview, I was able to discern how much money they pulled in, in terms of gross revenue per year (using the S.O.A.R. questioning criteria). I also asked how much they would like to be doing, and what would be a major breakthrough for them to accomplish in terms of gross revenue in the upcoming year. After I had all of this information I said to him, "Picture this, it's one year from now and your company has made 'X' millions of dollars, and you think to yourself, 'I'm sure glad I hired Chris because he's what made this happen for us.' Is that what you'd like to see happen?" He said, "Yes!" Understanding what was important to the company I was pitching (wants and values), I was then able to get them excited about my ability to satisfy those desires. I was hired for the job. The company almost tripled their sales the following year, a result far in excess of their previous expectations. In a meeting with the entire staff, the vice-president who has since become president, credited my training as the catalyst. The arrangement had served both of us well—a win-win, as I believe all sales should be. Make certain that you can back up your promises. This is the only way to build credibility, long-term relationships, repeat business, and ultimately attain your vision.

NEGOTIATING

Negotiation is crucial in sales as well as many walks of life. Whether you are negotiating with your partner to attend a workshop with you, or negotiating with your kids to take a share in the housework, or negotiating to buy a property or sell one million widgets, the skills of negotiation are imperative to your success. An extremely effective process for successful negotiating is detailed later in the chapter. First, it's important to be aware of the following tools for communicating your ideas.

THE AGREEMENT FRAME

The Agreement Frame is an elegant way to direct your conversation down the road you choose. It's really very simple: Never use the word "but" when attempting to persuade or get people to see your way of seeing. "But" is a negation operator in language, which means that when you use it in a sentence you negate everything that comes before it. For example, if you said, "I think this is what we should do," and I said, "Yes, but we can't," even though I answered with "yes," I then contradicted that positive response with "but," which effectively made it a negative response. You may get the sense your idea has been rejected and get defensive.

If, on the other hand I answered using "I agree and…" or "I respect and…" or I appreciate and…", it would have felt very different. So I could have said, "I appreciate that you are thinking of the best interests of the company and that's exactly why I think we should do it this way…" It's much more elegant, gets the same outcome, and sends the conversation in the direction of agreement. That is why it's called the Agreement Frame. Use it and notice how much smoother your negotiations go.

TECHNIQUES FOR GAINING SPECIFICITY IN NEGOTIATION

Chunking

"Chunking" refers to the fact that there are many different planes of abstraction that we can think and communicate on. Your ability to think on several levels of abstraction has a direct relation to your income level. Who has to think in more levels of abstraction, the CEO or the parking attendant? Who makes the larger income?

So when you are in negotiations with someone, chunking

can be a very useful tool in finding agreement that may not be immediately apparent.

ABSTRACTION TO DETAIL
Chunking Using the Hierarchy of Ideas

USEFUL FOR

Finding the intention behind the demand

Finding how to motivate others

Discovering new options

CHUNKING UP

Move from a specific term to the general category.

For Agreement, Alignment

CHUNKING DOWN

Move from the specific to the more specific or to the component parts.

For Specificity, the "How To"

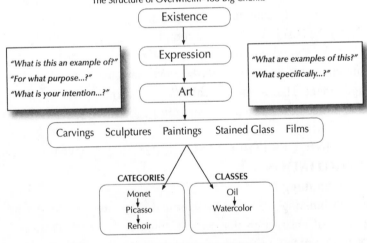

BIG PICTURE

Abstraction / Intuitor / Trance

The Structure of Overwhelm–Too Big Chunks

Existence

"What is this an example of?"
"For what purpose...?"
"What is your intention...?"

Expression

"What are examples of this?"
"What specifically...?"

Art

Carvings   Sculptures   Paintings   Stained Glass   Films

CATEGORIES

Monet
↓
Picasso
↓
Renoir

CLASSES

Oil
Watercolor

CHUNKING DOWN TO DETAILS

Chunking Up

Chunking up is when you move from a specific term to the general category. To chunk up on an idea you can ask a number of questions:

- What is this an example of?
- What is its purpose?
- What is your intention?

If you wanted to chunk up on the idea of "car" for example, you would ask the appropriate questions from the list above. What is a car an example of? What is the purpose of a car? What is the intention of the car? One answer to these questions could be "transportation." You have just chunked up to transportation, which is a more abstract idea than car. If you then wanted to chunk up further, you would repeat the process to get to "movement," etc.

Chunking Down

Chunking down is when you move from a general category to a specific term or from a specific term to a more specific term. To chunk down on an idea you can ask:

- What are examples of this?
- What specifically…?

So to chunk down on the same example you would ask, "What are examples of a car?" The answer to that could be either, classes and categories of cars such as Lexus, Subaru, etc., or it could be parts of a car such as wheel, hub cap, etc. Say for example, you went to the garage and said to the mechanic, "I have a problem with my car." The mechanic is going to chunk down to get more specific information that will direct him to the cause of the problem. So the conversation may go something like this:

You: "I have a problem with my car."

Mechanic: "What specifically is wrong with your car?"

You: "I don't know, it's something to do with the wheel"

Mechanic: "What specifically is wrong with the wheel?"
You: "It's something to do with the lug nuts."
Mechanic: What specifically is wrong with the lug nuts?"
You: "They are all missing."
Mechanic: "Ahh, well that's your problem."

By using this technique, which some people actually do naturally and can also be consciously used, the mechanic was able to isolate the problem and solve it. The same could also be done based on the type of car involved. For example, the mechanic would first clarify the make and model of the car so he or she could make an accurate assessment.

Lateral Chunking

You can also chunk laterally. To do this you would chunk up one level and then ask, "What are other examples of this?" So for the same example, if I were to chunk laterally on car, I would chunk up to transportation and then ask what are some other examples of transportation? The answer could be buses, boats, planes, trains, etc.

By practicing your ability to chunk up, down, and laterally you will find that you start to think circles around the people you are dealing with and negotiating with. This will assist you in ways you didn't think possible in terms of getting to your outcome.

Remember that the greater your ability to think in expanded planes of abstraction, the more money you will make in the world. The ability to think through the range from specific to abstract is one of the traits of extraordinary leaders, managers, and entrepreneurs. Abstract alone will not be nearly as effective as your ability to move through the range. Also, the person who controls the level of abstraction in a conversation controls the conversation.

From a negotiation standpoint there is always less disagreement the more you chunk up, so the more abstract an idea, the less room there is to disagree. And if you are able to gracefully achieve a positive response by dealing in the abstract first, you then create positive momentum, which assists in the final specific agreement.

For example, say you go into a business to help the two owners negotiate something. The first owner says, "We can't agree on anything and you can't help us agree on anything because we can't even agree on the color of the carpet in the hallway." You could then chunk up and say, "What's the purpose of your being in business? Is it to make a profit?" Both would likely have to agree with that. Subsequently, the idea that "we can't agree on anything" is immediately dissolved. By chunking up to a level of agreement, it is far easier to chunk back down and resolve the necessary issues.

In negotiation, once you have chunked up for agreement you would then only chunk back down again as quickly as you can maintain agreement. Knowing what the big picture outcome is, you can then use that in a conditional close to get final agreement.

A conditional close is when you say, "If we get you _____, then any way we get you that is OK? They would then say yes and you can start to move through the detail.

For example, if you've just gotten both partners to agree that they are in business to make a profit, you then say, "So if we were able to get you profitable, then anyway we get you that would be OK?" Once both have agreed, the details of how they will become profitable becomes much simpler to resolve.

PRECISION COMMUNICATION

A great tool to use for effective communication and negotiation, that will also help in the chunking process, is the Meta Model. The Meta Model is a framework to assist in clear communication. It can be a highly effective tool in bridging the understanding divide.

In the early 1970's, Dr. Richard Bandler and John Grinder, founders of Neuro Linguistic Programming (NLP), set out to determine how change was created in a successful therapeutic interaction, and how we could replicate that change without going through years of therapy. They started by breaking down the patterns of the most effective therapists in the world at the time. The first was Virginia Satir.

Satir was known for her ability to speak with someone quite conversationally, and as she did, she would simply gain specificity through her language. By gaining this specificity her patients would find that their problems would take on a different perspective. As a result, understanding between people was rapid and effective. Problems would melt away as the client would gain clarity about their own unique Rule Book, therefore the expectations and true meaning of their own and others' communication. An example of an interaction with Satir might go something like this:

Client:	"He hurt me."
Virginia Satir:	"How specifically?"
Client:	"Because he doesn't love me."
Virginia Satir:	"How do you know he doesn't love you?"
Client:	"Because when I come home he's always watching TV and not paying attention to me."
Virginia Satir:	"How specifically does his watching TV mean that he doesn't love you?"
Client:	"Well I guess it doesn't necessarily mean that."

In this case, the client was able to see that she had created a rule that for her to feel loved she must be the center of attention all the time. That's not logical. No one can be the center of someone's attention *all* the time. But until the questions were asked, the client wasn't aware of this internal belief.

Some of the patterns that Satir used were presented formally as the "Meta Model." This is a linguistic model used to retrieve information from individuals by gaining specificity. It also serves to enrich or widen an individual's "internal maps" by challenging the limits, or boundary conditions, of their Rule Book and brings their subconscious belief system into awareness.

The Meta Model is a way of dealing with the deletions, distortions, and generalizations that we talked about in Chapter four. Say for example someone said, "Everyone always forgets my birthday." This is a generalization that has disempowered the individual and made them feel unloved and sad. The words "everyone" and "always" represent the generalization that has been made.

The Meta Model teaches us a systematic way of bringing that person back to a more balanced reality. You may then ask, "Who specifically forgot your birthday?" "When specifically did they forget it?" By using this simple technique you can shift someone's perspective very quickly and easily.

The **basic** questions of the Meta Model are:
- What specifically?
- How specifically?
- When specifically?
- Where specifically?
- Who specifically?

We go much deeper into the Meta Model questioning techniques in some of our live trainings, but for now start with the basic questions for specificity listed above.

Practice both the chunking techniques and the Meta Model in your daily conversations and notice the difference it makes in understanding and rapport. You can even listen to conversations to see whether the speaker is chunking up, down, or laterally.

When you recognize how communication can stray off course or create misunderstandings due to people speaking from different chunking levels, you can then direct the conversation with volition in the direction that better serves both your objectives.

Two other powerful ways of gaining specificity and reducing the room for error in communication is through the following process.

1) Summation of points—Sum up the communication by checking your understanding of what has been said. For example, "Let me just make sure I have complete understanding of where we are in this communication. You feel that we should approach the project in a way which is more conservative, is that correct?"

2) Ask for feedback—The other way to close a loop is to ask the receiver for feedback. For example, "So based upon our discussion, what are you going to do differently or how specifically do you plan on approaching this?"

The meaning of the communication is the response it elicits. If you are not getting the result you want, you are not communicating effectively. Change your approach until you get your objective. Using these various techniques will prove extremely effective for determining the exact effect of your communication and keeping the flow of understanding between you.

Now you have the basis for powerful persuasive communication—let the negotiations begin!

NEGOTIATING

Negotiating is like traveling. Once you have determined your desired destination, you map out the best route to get there—preferably before you set off. If you run into any impasses or detours along the way, you simply find alternative routes. All roads are somehow connected so that if you were to put your finger on one spot anywhere on the map and someone else had their finger on another, you could find countless ways to get from one to the other. And before you can get to where you want to go, you always begin by preparing for your journey. Preparation is the first step before entering into any negotiations.

PRE-NEGOTIATION PREPARATION
1. Know your ideal outcome
You have to know exactly what you want before you can get it. So think ahead. Successful negotiation begins with successful planning. Ask yourself what your best possible resolution or ideal outcome would be.

2. Brainstorm all possible ways to arrive at this desired outcome
Be flexible. Maintaining a fixed position negates any possibility of forward movement right off the bat. A fixed position can be a stuck position. This leads to frustration and ultimately no one gets what they want. Explore your options. If there is more than one way (and there always is), then let your mind imagine all the alternatives. Whether you are negotiating for yourself or mediating between two people or groups, this flexibility of thinking is essential.

A caveat to this is you also need to know before you utter your first word what you would absolutely not accept and what you would settle for. In other words, decide on the boundaries beyond which you will not go, as well as those lines you are willing to cross.

3. Identify common goals
While still in the pre-negotiation stage, begin to look for areas on which both parties will probably agree. Once you have identified some common goals, you have your leverage. If negotiations ever begin to derail, you will be able to get things back on track by returning to these areas of alignment. These areas of

potential agreement will be your basis for beginning the actual negotiations. For a true win-win resolution each party must have at least one shared desired outcome. Without common outcomes, there is no place to begin because there is no place to end that will satisfy both. Always presume that both sides can win!

4. Recognize and plan for potential trouble spots

Obviously there are areas of disagreement or you wouldn't be negotiating. So the key here is to devise ways ahead of time that you could possibly approach and resolve those areas. This is where brainstorming all your alternative routes to the ideal solution will come in handy. How you bring them up in discussion will also be important.

5. Choose your best path to your ideal outcome

Now that you have prepared yourself for every possible aspect of the coming negotiation, decide which option you will present first. Even keep in mind the possibility that none of the problems you have considered will present themselves and you may arrive at your win-win quicker than you thought.

SUCCESSFUL NEGOTIATING

Once discussions begin, the most effective route to win-win solutions follows these three stages:

STAGE 1) Find Common Ground
1. Establish rapport

This should be the first step to any human interaction. However, it is especially useful in negotiating because it creates the much-needed atmosphere of responsiveness and trust that keeps people working together toward a common vision.

2. Clarify agreed-upon outcome

Have both sides state their goals. If it seems there is little common ground, keep redefining what you really want and what that will mean to each party. Then pay close attention to the words used. We all use language differently, so it's very possible you do have shared goals yet state them differently. Listen for ideas you can chunk up or down on to arrive at the common goal(s) you might not have recognized. Again, you have no chance for resolution without common goals, so persist until you find some. Move on to the next step only when you have clarified both sides' agreed-upon outcome.

3. State conditional close

"Conditional close" is a term most often used in sales. However, it is an invaluable tool for negotiating as it quickly and invariably moves people closer to clarity, resolution, and commitment. It's a linguistic devise in which you simply ask someone to suppose the desired outcome by using, "Just suppose…" or "If… then…" For example, if you are mediating between a chain of stores and their striking employees and have determined that both sides agree they want to get back to work to keep the company running, you could ask, "Just suppose we reached agreement on the outstanding issues, then would you agree to get back to work?" This is the most effective way to move through a stalemate because it reminds all parties of their shared agreement and immediately brings focus to what is needed for a solution.

STAGE 2) Move Beyond Differences

4. Clarify areas to be resolved

At this stage not only are both sides united on common ground, everyone also recognizes the common destination. The only question remaining is which route to take to get everyone there. It's time to clarify and highlight exactly what those roadblocks are.

5. Uncover intention behind areas of disagreement

This is the most crucial and essential stage (and where negotiating is most fun) where you use your skills of chunking up and down to arrive at the true intention behind both sides' stated demands. For example, a workers union is in negotiations with management. The union says they want a higher hourly wage for their members. On probing it is discovered that the reason for this is so that members will not have to work such long hours, because they want to spend more time with their families. By uncovering this intention the management then has an option to satisfy the requirement without necessarily having to give the pay increase. They could, for example, give more vacation time, or move shifts around for those with families so they get to spend more time with their families. This step is very useful because it gets to the intent behind the request so that both parties can see that there might be a different way to meet their objectives.

It requires you to probe by chunking up and asking, "And you want that for what purpose?"

6. Chunk down while maintaining agreement

Gradually chunk back down until you have returned to those specific areas that require resolution. Every time you reach disagreement, chunk back up until both sides agree. Then move back down through the trouble spots with the conditional close again, this time using more specific terms. For example, "If we got you (x,y,z) then any way you get that will be okay?" They will usually say yes because their focus is on the "what" more than the "how." Your job is the "how."

7. Present options

This is the point you present some of the ways everyone could get the intention behind their original demands. They have already told you that they would accept any way that they could get their desired results, so anything you propose should be acceptable. Because you did your pre-negotiation preparation, you will have several options up your sleeve to choose from. Get their ideas too and ask for their preferences. These will be the actual terms upon which you will soon find yourselves agreeing.

STAGE 3) Resolution

8. Confirm agreement

Decide on the best option and move to close.

9. Specify action plan

Now you are arriving at your common destination together. Summarize the detailed action plan, making sure you keep agreement through the details. Repeat steps 4-7 until both parties confirm resolution. End with the first step you each need to take next.

You have just learned how to exquisitely handle any negotiations, whether you are negotiating your own contract, mediating for others as a business consultant, or sorting out differences within your own team or family. Combined with the Win-Win Selling process, you now have all the steps you need to arrive at buying commitments in any context, whether buying into a proposal, a product, or a vision for the future. This will serve you well in leading people toward your own vision with power and influence. That is what we will cover next.

SIXTEEN

How to Communicate with Power

"Leadership appears to be the art of getting others to want to do something you are convinced should be done."

~ Vance Packard

There are several laws and principles which when followed can assist you in creating maximum power and influence in your world. As with all powerful information, these principles are open to abuse. The tools themselves are ethic-less. People have ethics. A scalpel can be used to heal or harm. I ask that you use these principles only to create win-win outcomes for you and those you work with.

Cialdini's Principles

In his book *Influence–The Psychology of Persuasion*, Robert Cialdini Ph.D., proposes six universal principles that are prevalent in human influence. These include reciprocation, social validation, commitment and consistency, friendship and liking, scarcity, and authority.

Cialdini discovered these principles by studying human behavior in a number of situations and noticing the major patterns of influence. This must-read book discusses the psychology of what makes people do the things they do.

Reciprocity

Put in its simplest form, this is the need to address the balance. If someone gives you something, there is an innate need or desire to return the gift. This law works in all relationships to some extent of another. If you have a friendship and you always seem to give more to that friendship than you receive, sooner or later, the friendship will dissolve because there was no "give and take" between you.

This technique is used widely in marketing with free gifts and memberships, which hook the customer in and activate the law of reciprocity. Cialdini details how the Hare Krishnas used this law spectacularly in the 1970s as a fundraising technique. They would give passersby a flower. That's it! A harmless little flower. No money was requested. However, this innate principal is so strong that even though the recipients didn't necessarily want the flower, the need to repay the debt of kindness in some way resulted in the generation of millions of dollars.

Whatever you give out in life you tend to get back sooner or later. So if you go through life looking for the good in others and helping people get what they need and want, whether there is instant reward in it or not, reciprocity will prevail somewhere along the line.

Social Validation

Cialdini refers to this law as social proof. This is simply the comfort and acceptance that comes from seeing others do the same things we're doing. People are innately comforted if they are part of a pack. There is a feeling of acceptance and belonging gained by being like other people.

Again, marketers and salespeople have found ways to initiate this law simply by adding testimonials from people "just like you" who have bought and loved their product.

If you can make people feel comfortable and happy through your communication, then your results will reflect this. By activating the law of social proof you can make others feel at ease.

Commitment and Consistency

This is the need to remain consistent with an identity we

have created for ourselves. Once we have been seen to make a decision or take a stand about something we will experience pressure to behave consistently with that choice.

No one likes to admit they were wrong, and this is basically that premise taken to an extreme. Rather than admit a mistake, most people will maintain a particular course even though in their heart of hearts they know it is not the correct thing to do.

Again the world of marketing has tapped into this by asking questions in sales that lead a person into the buying decision. This is not always a bad thing, but it is good to be aware of the power of these influencers so you can guard against their unscrupulous use. There are times where their use is valuable and will lead to win-win outcomes all around.

Take the time to understand what motivates other people and speak to them in their own language. This is why values elicitation is so useful. It can allow you to tap into a person's natural motivators and make a positive impact while also giving them what they need.

Liking

This one is fairly obvious. You do business with people you like. This is why rapport skills are so imperative. The famous trial attorney Clarence Darrow once said, "The true job of a trial attorney is to get the jury to like their client."

In fact, in most court room situations the jury will make an initial evaluation and decision as to the guilt or innocence of the defendant within the first five minutes. All the information that comes in after that point will go to substantiate the decision they have already made about that defendant's guilt or innocence. The jurors will actually delete information that does not corroborate their initial decision of his or her guilt or innocence.

Be someone you would like to be around. Have fun, laugh, be polite, friendly, and optimistic and you'll be surprised how people will warm to you. And if people like you they will listen to you. If they listen, they may hear what you have to propose.

Authority – The Power of Prestige

This is the sort of power a doctor wields in a white coat. We place huge importance on information given from authority figures. There is a level of trust that is given to them that seems to even bypass the individual need to validate that authority.

We are so accustomed to listening and responding to people of authority and are therefore, apt to alter our behavior as a result of a suggestion from them. Marketers have used this to great effect by getting celebrity endorsement or testimonials from "qualified professionals." For example, health supplements may be endorsed by a famous athlete and accompanied by a testimonial from a leading nutritionist.

In hypnosis, there is a concept called the "prestige suggestion." A prestige suggestion is any suggestion accepted by someone simply because of the level of prestige of the person who delivered it. Ninety percent of hypnosis is prestige. People will often follow the suggestions simply because they are delivered from "a hypnotist." It works the same way in the field of medicine. You have heard, no doubt, of the placebo effect. This is a result of the prestige suggestion that comes from the doctor and the "legitimacy" of the medication provided. The more prestige or authority we acquire, the more our interpersonal suggestions and communications will be heeded.

In the 19th Century, Franz Anton Mesmer became famous for his ability to heal sick or diseased people by mesmerizing them. He was so successful that at one point there were thousands of people a day coming to see him. He would pass his hands over them, their eyes would roll back in their heads, and they would go into convulsions. Then they would be healed. This worked very well for him until a commission was empowered by the politicians and the doctors in an attempt to "debunk" him and prove him a fake. Three people served on this commission, the French chemist Lavoisiere, a French specialist in pain control named Guillotine, and the American Benjamin Franklin. Mesmer claimed to heal people through a magnetic energy that flowed forth from his hands. In his report back to the French government, Benjamin Franklin said, "I cannot see this mesmeric energy of which he speaks, and therefore, he must be a fake." As a result, Mesmer lost his prestige and authority and many of the people who he had previously healed became sick again. This story is not only a reminder of the power of authority but the power of beliefs.

Scarcity

Here's a paradox of life—social proof states that we feel comfort if other people are doing what we are doing, i.e. there is safety in numbers. Yet scarcity says we are also influenced by the need to be different—to stand out from the crowd!

An opportunity will always seem more valuable if there is an element of scarcity to it. Open any magazine and see "Limited offer—must close Sunday!" or "Limited edition collector's item—only 2 left!" This feeling that we may miss out on something special and unique will drive us to take action.

These are some of the hallmarks of powerful communication, so understand their innate ability to influence and bring them into your communication when appropriate. As you continue to expand your Game, you will need to enroll the efforts of other players in your team to reach your objectives. Life is not a solo sport even though many of us would like to think it could be. It involves assisting others to achieve their dreams too. This requires vision and leadership.

SEVENTEEN

The Art of Spin and Masterful Story Telling: How to Shift Perceptions Through Language

*"Learning the game of power requires
a certain way of looking at the world,
a shifting of perspective."*
~ Robert Greene

When I was younger, I traveled all over the world–to Mexico where I rode horses through the desert, Greece and Turkey where I saw wondrous underwater sunken cities. I explored caves in the Italian islands and the British West Indies. I went wreck diving in St. Barts and shark feeding in Tahiti. I was always interested in seeing the world from every possible viewpoint. It was this that excited me, because I was always so curious as to how to see things differently. In this chapter, you will learn some of the most powerful techniques on the planet for expanding people's perceptions, and shifting viewpoints while getting your point across.

An event is not inherently good or bad, right or wrong. Judgments and evaluations we make about events are subjective, based completely upon our individual model of the world. Because no two people have exactly the same model of the world, people's interpretations of outside events can't help but be biased. The observer always and intimately effects the observed.

Mother Theresa received criticism for feeding the hungry instead of teaching them how to feed themselves. She was therefore doing the hungry a disservice by feeding them, which is a fair and valid opinion. Many, if not most, of the people in the world would say she was doing them a huge service, which is also a fair and valid belief. The event did not change, just the perspective on the event and how it was "spun."

The art of spin is shifting the frame of perception around something to alter the evaluation of it. Spin to some extent is the human manifestation of what we talked about at the beginning of the book—the Universe changes based on who and what is looking at it. The world of Mother Theresa was viewed very differently depending on who was looking at it!

Spin is a relatively new term and is used frequently in politics and marketing. A great example of political spin occurred in the Presidential primary debates between Walter Mondale and Ronald Reagan. At the time, Mondale was pushing the point that Reagan was too old to run for President. At one point in the debate, the moderator asked Ronald Reagan if he thought that age should be made an issue in the debate. Ronald Reagan replied, "No. I don't think it should be an issue. I refuse to make an issue of my opponent's youth and inexperience."

This was a fantastic use of spin—he turned the whole argument on its head and rather than defend his age he used the same line from a different angle. He targeted his opponent's "youth and inexperience," which shifted the frame of reference, therefore turning an attack around to be utterly ineffective.

Henry Kissinger once opened a press conference by saying, "Who has the questions to the answers I've prepared?" The point being he was a master of delivering the message he intended to deliver. No matter how a question was posed he could turn it around to his advantage. Although the term "spin" has more recently been given a somewhat negative *spin*, it is just another word for reframing, or offering a new perspective.

S.P.I.N. P.A.T.T.E.R.N.

One of the easy acronyms to remember when using persuasive language is the S.P.I.N. P.A.T.T.E.R.N.S., explained below:

Spin Patterns

There are many linguistic patterns that we can use to assist us in changing people's perceptions. Why would we want to shift someone's perception, you might ask. Well, would you like to know how to assist people to see your perspective? To take up a cause? Make your point hit home at a company meeting? What if you could respond to any objection or argument and persuade people to see things differently? Consciously or not, some of our greatest leaders used these techniques, including Dr. Martin Luther King Jr. and Nelson Mandela.

Here are twelve different patterns that can totally change the way people view anything:

1) **S. Shift** to a larger frame
2) **P. Perspective** of others
3) **I. Importance** of higher values
4) **N. Negative** consequences

5) **P. Point** out a higher level of abstraction
6) **A. Analogy** or metaphor
7) **T. Transcend** the generalization
8) **T. Turn** to another issue
9) **E. Evaluation**
10) **R. Reversal**
11) **N. Newly** define
12) **S. Separate** intention from behavior

Let's take two separate beliefs or opinions and see how we would use each of the spin patterns to help that person see their belief from another perspective. Here are two statements for example and possible responses to them:

    a) "I'll never be successful because I have a learning disability."

    b) "I can't take your seminar because it's too expensive."

S. Shift to a Larger Frame: To generate this spin pattern, it's important to realize that for someone to hold the belief or generalization they currently have, they must be looking at the event or belief through a certain sized frame. By widening the frame size to include things they were not previously aware of or have not yet noticed, we can change the meaning of the event or belief within their thinking. A simple way to do this is to ask yourself, "What is a larger frame or something they haven't noticed which, when noticed, will cause their position to change?" Here are some ways to spin these objections:

    a) "I'll never be successful because I have a learning disability."
        Response: "You're just saying that because you haven't researched all the people with similar challenges who have become massively successful."

    b) "I can't take your seminar because it's too expensive."
        Response: "Once you've taken a look at our tuition financing options you'll understand how affordable it can really be."

P. Perspective of Others: Remember that no two people share the same model of the world. To alter another person's perspective you need to recognize any generalization and show how it could be viewed differently, from another's perspective. Apply these responses to the same two objections:

a) "I'll never be successful because I have a learning disability."

Response: "Many people - myself included - don't believe in learning disabilities... just in ineffective learning strategies. And learning strategies can be changed."

b) "I can't take your seminar because it's too expensive."

Response: "Our graduates understand that what was really expensive was the time they wasted before gaining the insights in our program."

I. Importance of Higher Values: Events have no inherent meaning until they are passed through an individual's Rule Book as we discussed earlier. One of the major factors for interpretation of events is our values. During the Monica Lewinski scandal, two political parties, which represent different sets of nationally held values, were viewing the same situation and placing a different meaning on it. One of the very effective spin patterns used throughout the course of the scandal by President Clinton and the Democratic Party was that of the *importance of higher values*. Wasn't it *more important* to get back to the work of the country? To be forgiving as a people? Wasn't it *more important* that he was such an effective President, and wasn't the great state of the economy *more important* than what occurred in his personal life? According to them, within their values, it was.

The way to tap into the power of the higher values pattern is to figure out their relevant values and then ask, "What is a higher universally held value?" or "What is a higher held value for the individual I'm communicating with that, when brought to his or her awareness, would result in a change in meaning?" Using the same example, here is a way to respond by using a higher value:

a) "I'll never be successful because I have a learning disability."

Response: "Isn't it more important to believe in yourself than to create reasons or excuses for your lack of success?"

b) "I can't take your seminar because it's too expensive."

Response: "Aren't you worth investing in?"

N. Negative Consequences: Shift the attention to the negative consequences of holding onto their generalization. This alters their perception.

a) "I'll never be successful because I have a learning disability."

Response: "It's beliefs like that that keep people from ever rising above their challenges."

b) "I can't take your seminar because it's too expensive."

Response: "What's it going to cost you if you don't do it? What is the price—physically, emotionally and financially?"

P. Point Out a Higher Level of Abstraction: This pattern can be utilized to bring into their mind exaggerated or larger patterns.

a) "I'll never be successful because I have a learning disability."

Response: "Many people have excuses for not succeeding in life. For some it's their sex, race, or creed, and for others it's a challenge such as yours. It's not that successful people don't have challenges. Successful people rise above their challenges."

b) "I can't take your seminar because it's too expensive."

Response: "Thoughts like that serve only to keep people from learning the tools that can change their lives for the better."

A. Analogy or Metaphor: Answer the generalization, objection, or event with an appropriate analogy or a metaphor.

   a) "I'll never be successful because I have a learning disability."

     Response: "I used to think it took me longer to learn
things than most people, and it was that very belief that
caused me to work even harder and propel myself on to
greater success."

   b) "I can't take your seminar because it's too expensive."

     Response: "Jon Andre Bliss said the same thing, but
then he realized it was too expensive not to do it. He
attended the course and within 30 days he had virtually
tripled his sales."

T. Transcend the Generalization: This pattern could also
be called "breaking the generalization." Shift attention to a time
when their generalization was not true.

   a) "I'll never be successful because I have a learning disability."

     Response: "Richard Branson was told he was dyslexic
and that didn't stop him from becoming a billionaire."

   b) "I can't take your seminar because it's too expensive."

     Response: "Too expensive compared to what? Com-
pared to the cost of not having this information? You pay
for education once. You pay for ignorance over and over
again."

T. Turn to another issue: Bring to their attention what you
believe to be really at issue. This pattern is frequently used in
politics. When Al Gore asked for a recount of the Florida votes
and was first granted it, he said, "It's not a victory for Al Gore,
but a victory for our Democracy."

   a) "I'll never be successful because I have a learning disability."

Response: "The issue isn't whether you *can* become successful, the issue is whether you *are willing* to become successful despite the challenges you're confronted with."

b) "I can't take your seminar because it's too expensive."

Response: "The issue isn't the amount of the investment. The issue is how much you think you're worth investing in."

E. Evaluation: People make their own evaluations based on their model of the world and then label things as meaning one thing or another. This pattern will allow them to see their own assumptions, then alter their interpretation and consider new possibilities.

a) "I'll never be successful because I have a learning disability."

Response: "Your success is not determined by your challenges. Your success is determined by your commitments."

b) "I can't take your seminar because it's too expensive."

Response: "The price of the seminar doesn't mean you can't attend, it simply means you've got to commit yourself to your own success. Where there's a will there's a way."

R. Reversal: Utilize their reasoning to show them that the very reason they gave the objection is the same reason they should take the action you prescribe. This pattern is used quite frequently in sales. When someone says, "It costs too much, I can't afford it," the salesperson responds with, "That's why you have to do it."

a) "I'll never be successful because I have a learning disability."

Response: "That's exactly why you need to become successful... so you can prove to yourself and others how powerful you can be when you decide to overcome something."

b) "I can't take your seminar because it's too expensive."
   Response: "That's exactly why you need to do whatever you have to in order to attend. How long do you want to go on not being able to afford the things you really want in life?"

N. Newly Define: This pattern gives an alternate definition they may not have thought about, therefore opens their eyes to a different way of seeing something, or redefines their perceptions.

a) "I'll never be successful because I have a learning disability."
   Response: "Success is not something that is achieved by having no challenges. Success is the process of overcoming your challenges."

b) "I can't take your seminar because it's too expensive."
   Response: "Our program is not expensive, it's valuable. How much would you pay for something that helped you to double your income? That's exactly what Christine Winters did after attending."

S. Separate Intention from Behavior: This pattern is used to separate intention from behavior so that someone can see where one is not supporting the other.

a) "I'll never be successful because I have a learning disability."
   Response: "I know your intention is to keep yourself from experiencing disappointment, but how disappointed would you be if you got to the end of your life and you

never reached your full potential because of that lousy excuse?"

b) "I can't take your seminar because it's too expensive."
Response: "I know that you're interested in making wise financial decisions and we've got lots of clients that will assure you this is one of the smartest financial decisions you could make."

These spin patterns are some of the fastest and most effective ways to influence others positively. I have a lot of fun with these because using language in this way with the other person's best interest in mind instantly expands their perspective. With your developed sensory acuity, you can almost literally watch people's thinking begin to change direction. The best responses cause a person to reflect on their assumptions and beliefs implicit in the words they choose. Whether you are going to an investor for a business loan or talking with your teenager, instead of dreading objections to your proposal, you can now look at their responses as a wide open opportunity to expand their thinking.

STORIES AND ANALOGIES

"People need stories more than bread itself.
They tell us how to live and why."
~ Arabian Nights

Stories and analogies are another powerful way of expressing your ideas, teaching, and assisting people to see the world in new ways. Storytelling is an essential tool in getting a team moving forward congruently toward the accomplishment of noble objectives. The best teachers of all time have been able to communicate in ways that simplify grand ideas by correlating their message through some other event or situation. Some of the greatest movements that have ever graced the planet have been accomplished with the help of charismatic leaders who knew the power of communicating through metaphor and analogy. Martin Luther King Jr. was one such leader who possessed this power of persuasive storytelling. There are also leaders within the world of business who have made a tremendous impact on people using metaphor.

Warren Buffett's primary mentor Benjamin Graham, the grandfather of value investing, used the now famous metaphor of Mr. Market to explain how to be an outstanding investor. He said to imagine that as an investor, you are in business with a manic-depressive partner who goes through huge mood swings on a daily basis. One moment he's telling you business is great and he quotes you a price for which he's willing to buy you out. A few hours later his sunny outlook disappears and he's all gloom and doom, trying to tell you your company is now worth next to nothing so you should sell now, while you still can. The best time to buy is actually when he's overly pessimistic and desperate to sell, not when he's being overly optimistic, when everyone else is buying. To this day Buffett often recalls the story of Mr. Market when making investment decisions, especially if he's ever tempted to get fearful when others are fearful.

Children's books and movies are also full of important life lessons presented as metaphors wrapped within the plots and story lines. Walt Disney movies are well known for this. Take for example the movie *The Lion King*. A young lion cub named Simba is playing outside the safe area. Simba gets into trouble and his father goes to the rescue only to be killed himself by the Hyenas.

Simba is distraught and runs away from the pride in shame. He goes off to live with other animals in a far away part of the forest. Several years later a childhood friend of Simba's comes to find him because an evil tyrannical leader has taken charge of the pride and Simba is the only one who can defeat him.

When she asks Simba to return, Simba says that he can never return because of what happened in the past. One of Simba's newfound friends, a wise-old sage and monkey named Rafiki, goes to speak with him. "Why can you not go back and take your rightful place?" asks Rafiki. "Because of what happened in the past," replies Simba sadly. At that point, Rafiki raps Simba across the head with his walking stick. Simba yelps in pain and demands, "What was that for?" Referring to the stick, he says, "It does not matter... it's in the past." Simba sees the connection and that Rafiki is helping him see that it wasn't his fault.

Then Rafiki goes to hit Simba again and this time Simba ducks. The message is that what is important about the past is to get the lessons and teachings so that we can change our behaviors in the future to produce the results that we want. Its purpose is not to limit us, but rather to teach and instruct us—a profound lesson presented within a children's tale.

THE PURPOSE OF STORIES

The main purpose of storytelling is to bypass conscious resistance to teaching or making a point. Because we come into every conversation with a set of our own ideas and meanings, it is sometimes difficult to get someone to see a certain perspective because they are emotionally attached to their existing one.

By dissociating the individual or group from any given situation, it is possible to lead them to a "solution" for a particular problem or situation without implicating or blaming anyone. That's what happens therapeutically with a story. It works well that way, because when someone is stuck in a problem they tend to have quite a bit of feeling and energy contained within it. When you walk up to someone like that and say, "Here's your solution," it's usually not very effective. But if you can represent the issue they are currently experiencing through a seemingly unrelated experience you can open up a neural pathway that can lead to a new perspective and understanding. The person hearing the story gets the connection between the story and their own experience. They can then go on to make the internal connection and solve their problem.

From a quantum biology point of view, what you are doing is creating new neural networks inside the individual, which lead ultimately to new ways of viewing the world, and therefore new behavior.

ANALOGIES

An analogy is used to simplify communication by drawing a relationship between two things that had no prior relationship. It can assist someone to see a similarity between something they are already familiar with and something they are not. This makes them more comfortable with, able to relate to, or better understand any idea you are trying to get across. It can also be used like a story to really drive home a point or to assist people to see things in new ways.

The key to making an analogy work is to go from the known to the unknown. When Jesus spoke of becoming "fishers of men," that was an example of a superb analogy that allowed his audience to "bridge" the gap between what they already understood—fishing—and what they didn't—their purpose. The analogy gets the listener to transfer their positive associations with what's familiar to the vision or information you're relaying.

After studying many of the most influential communicators of all time, I have found one of the most eloquent and inspirational to be Dr. Martin Luther King, Jr.

Note the use of analogy in this excerpt from Dr. Martin Luther King's famous "I Have a Dream" speech:

"In a sense we have come to our nation's capitol to cash a check. When the architects of our republic wrote the magnificent words of the Constitution and the Declaration of Independence,

they were signing a promissory note to which every American was to fall heir. This note was a promise that all men would be guaranteed the unalienable rights of life, liberty, and the pursuit of happiness.

It is obvious today that America has defaulted on this promissory note insofar as her citizens of color are concerned. Instead of honoring this sacred obligation, America has given the Negro people a bad check—a check which has come back marked "insufficient funds." But we refuse to believe that the bank of justice is bankrupt. We refuse to believe that there are insufficient funds in the great vaults of opportunity of this nation. So we have come to cash this check—a check that will give us upon demand the riches of freedom and the security of justice."

Analogies work best when they meet one of two criteria. They are either 1) universal experiences, meaning that anybody can relate to them, or 2) tailor designed for the individual based on their interests and values.

I was working with a 9 year-old boy who had been branded Attention Deficit Hyperactivity Disorder (A.D.H.D.). (by the way, I don't subscribe to the concept of learning disabilities, although I do believe that there are inflexible teachers and communicators.) I'll call the boy Jonathan for the purposes of this story. Jonathan's parents had tried everything to calm him down and get him to pay attention in class, to no avail. They called me in to work with him and I showed up at his house to meet him one day. When I met Jonathan, he really was bouncing off the walls. He would switch from topic to topic as we spoke incessantly. His shoes were off, so I took mine off too, and then I began to match and mirror his overt physiology. Once I had sufficient rapport, I slowed down and then noticed that he began to follow my lead and slow down himself.

At this point, I asked him about how he did in school. "I

don't do very well, because I have A.D.H.D.," he replied. I asked him what he really liked and enjoyed doing when he was not at school. He told me that he loved to do gymnastics. When I asked him to tell me more about that, his physiology and energy changed dramatically. His focus shifted completely, and for the first time since I had begun speaking with him he was able to stay on topic. He told me about various competitions he had been in and how much he truly loved it. So then I asked him about how he learned to do gymnastics, and he continued with much pride and excitement to describe the process. Then I commented on *how much fun it sounded to learn* and began to assist him in linking learning to fun through our conversation.

One thing I notice with children who are labeled A.D.H.D. is that they seem to be able to pay attention to things that they like and enjoy. It's often only when they don't like something or they lack commitment to something that they exhibit unruly behavior. I asked Jonathan what else he really enjoyed doing and he mentioned that he liked to sit on his deck and watch the dolphins in the ocean. So the two of us went up on the deck and watched the dolphins together. Once again his focus and attention were fixated. I explained to him, while we sat there, how easy it was to really focus in on things. We went back inside and I asked him if he would like to learn how to keep the teachers off his back, get better grades, make his classes at school go by a lot faster, and be able to spend more time doing gymnastics instead of homework.

He let me know that would suit him just fine. Then I taught him how to go into the learning state (the state of expanded awareness you learned earlier). I told him it was similar to dolphin watching. Just like he was watching a dolphin in the ocean, he could focus on a spot just above eye level and then allow his vision to expand out into the peripheral. He went swiftly and easily into the learning state, and soon it became quite easy for him to slow down and focus anytime he chose.

At the end of our time together, I explained that whenever he wanted to, he could simply go into the learning state and his class time would pass by very quickly and the information being taught in class would just go right inside his head and he would remember everything easily. The learning state in this case serves as a waking type of hypnotic trance, which is quite useful in learning and retaining information.

By transferring the fun of learning gymnastics—something he was quite familiar with—to learning in general, he was able to experience beyond the belief instilled in him that he wasn't good at learning. The analogy of watching a dolphin was also used and made it easier for Jonathan to focus and pay attention. What makes the analogy work is to go from the known to the unknown. In this particular case, it also provided new resources that Jonathan didn't know he had.

HOW TO CREATE STORIES

The construction of stories can range from simplistic to quite complex, yet regardless of complexity they can be incredibly powerful in solving problems for others or assisting them to think about things in new ways.

In order to construct a story, all that is necessary is to find a situation or circumstance that parallels the concept you'd like to illustrate. For the purposes of explaining story construction, I will describe how to create them in the context of creating behavioral change. I find that by explaining them this way you will understand the finer intricacies that go into designing metaphors better and that can have an incredible impact on the consciousness of the other person. This serves to give a deeper understanding of the construction, and then, once the intricacies are understood, you can take the patterns taught and apply them cross contextually in business, leadership, sales, activism, coaching, or education.

CONSTRUCTING A STORY TO CREATE CHANGE OR GET SOMEONE TO TAKE ACTION

A) Find out what the problem state or current situation is and determine in your own mind the solution. It is also beneficial at this point to determine what is preventing the other person from having the solution.

B) Chunk up on the problem or current situation (in the same way you learned in the Negotiating section). Ask yourself, "What is their situation an example of?"

C) Chunk laterally by asking yourself, "What are other examples of this?"

D) Using one of these examples, tell a story about someone or something in a similar situation who resolved the problem OR discovered resources they didn't realize they had. Another way is to end the story with the negative consequences of not taking action.

You can create change within an individual, on both a thinking and behavioral level, and ultimately get them to take a desired action using story. Let's take a look at each step of the process of story construction.

A. What is the Problem?

The first step is to find out what the problem state or current situation is, then determine the best possible solution. Either ask the person directly or ask yourself, "Where are they now? And where would they like to be instead?" Once you understand the issues it's important to really associate with it yourself so you fully appreciate the situation and come up with a story that will deeply affect the listener in a way that will cause them to more easily solve their own "problem."

Let's say for example that you know someone who wants to increase his business, but feels he can't really expand because he believes he doesn't have the money it would take. You know it's necessary for him to think outside the box of his current thinking in order to come up with some creative financing solutions. This solution may be better delivered in a story. Some people will undoubtedly ask, "if you already know the solution, why not just tell the person straight out?" Because by using a story, the person is prompted to search for his or her own meaning and to come to the solution in his or her own mind. This makes the process inductive, which is far more powerful than simply handing them the solution. They arrive at the solution themselves, therefore claim it and are more likely to act upon it.

B. What is this problem an example of?

The second step of the process is to "chunk up" on the problem or current situation. The idea is to get more abstract on the essence of their stated quandary. To see the problem in a bigger context, ask yourself, "What is this current problem an example of?" It could be an example of "feeling stuck" or "without options." It could also be an example of "rigid thinking" or "a lack of creative ideas." In this step, your job is to pick the concept you chunk up to that you feel most closely resembles the nature of the issue. In this case, let's say you decided that the problem is an example of "feeling stuck."

C. Where are there parallel examples of this problem?

The third step now is to chunk laterally, or think of examples that would demonstrate the larger concept you arrived at. In this case, after chunking up to "feeling stuck," the next question to ask is, "what are some *other* examples of feeling stuck?" It needs to be something the listener can relate to that would also be useful to lead the listener to a powerful solution. In this case, it could be traffic, being stuck on the freeway, standing on a line at a busy amusement park that isn't moving, or even a business story of someone you know who was in a similar situation that ended positively. There are plenty of answers other then those, by the way. They were simply the ones that came to mind for me at the time.

D. Tell a Parallel Story to Solve the Problem

The final step of the process of story construction is to create the story–using one of the examples that you created from step C, find a scenario that "bridges" the gap between the problem and the solution. Remember, the key to an effective outcome is using a character who either solves the problem within the story or discovers necessary resources he didn't know he had. While it is not absolutely necessary, the story is most effective when the person can immediately see the correlations between their situation and the story. For those who don't like to be told what to do or think, you can make your story more abstract so that they don't quite make the connection consciously. The higher you chunk up to abstraction in your story the more deeply subconscious the story's effect is. Here is how the process breaks down for this last example.

A person you are helping tells you he's frustrated because he wants to increase his business but he believes he can't expand because he doesn't have the marketing dollars it would take:

- A) Problem or current situation: "can't grow business"
  Solution: think outside the box
- B) An example of: feeling stuck
- C) Other examples of feeling stuck: standing in a long line at an amusement park, a car stuck in traffic, someone in a similar situation who increased their business
- D) **Story told**: Richard Branson growing Virgin Airlines

Here is a story that I could tell to this person. I have bolded the words here that I might emphasize while telling it:

"Richard Branson, founder of the Virgin Companies, didn't have much of a marketing budget when he launched Virgin Airlines. And he **felt a bit stuck at the time** because he knew that they needed to get the word out about the new airline. So one day he was **desperately trying to figure out what to do**, and he stopped and said to himself, '**No problem is insurmountable. You can do this. You've just got to think outside the box.**' Now, he knew that publicity which can often be free was worth many times the value of advertising, so he decided to **find a way** to get the publicity without paying the advertising dollars. Branson did it with a transatlantic crossing in the Virgin Challenger boat in an attempt to beat the speed record, which he failed on his first attempt. Nonetheless, the publicity that was created was enormous, which drove many people to his new airline. Now, I'm not saying that you have to be that extreme, but **certainly thinking outside of the box can lead to new solutions** that perhaps didn't even exist as possibilities to a mind that wasn't searching for them."

The Distinctions That Make Them Work

There are many distinctions that cause a story to work or to make an impact in someone's thinking, and therefore have the potential of actually affecting or changing behavior. The first and most important aspect is that the story must be intimately linked to that person's values. By constructing and delivering a story that holds importance to the person or group you're communicating with, you will captivate their attention.

Other distinctions we can add to the construction of stories to add impact are as follows:

1) Create a direct relationship between a character or characters in the story and the person or persons you are communicating with.
2) If possible use objects, circumstances, or other real life

people familiar with the person you are communicating with. Anything that adds familiarity within the story will draw them in and assist them to connect with it. In Martin Luther King's speech, he compared racial inequality to the writing of a bad check.

3) Use a story that relates to something that holds significance to the person. Jesus spoke to the fishermen of becoming fishers of men.

4) Use embedded commands and direct quotes inside the context of the story to ensure important points stand out, or to deliver a specific message. A direct quote is delivering a message to the person you are telling the story to through a character in the story. For example, in the Branson story where Richard Branson says to himself, **"No problem is insurmountable. You can do this. You've just got to think outside the box,"** the direct quote can be delivered lower and louder with tonal emphasis so that it stands out from the rest of the story making the most impact to the listener. A direct command is a command that is given overtly to another. A statement such as "Close the door" is an example of a direct command. These types of commands can also be "hidden" or "embedded" within a question or a statement to soften the "commanding" aspect, but to nevertheless deliver a very specific message that stands out in the mind of the person or group with whom you are communicating. An example of this would be: "I'm wondering how soon you'll... **close the door.**" The final part of the statement is delivered lower and with tonal emphasis.

5) Remember, you do not necessarily have to provide the solution outright in the story, or explain the meaning of your story. Instead, you may sometimes want to leave it open enough to cause the person or group to search for

the meaning and come to his or her own solutions. This becomes incredibly powerful, as they will still be making new connections long after you have told it. Plus, they may make associations that you never even thought of—so it's often extremely powerful to leave it up to them.

EIGHTEEN

Golden Rules for Success

"It is impossible for a man to conceal himself.
In every act, word or gesture he stands revealed as he is,
and not as he would have himself appear to be.
From the Universe, nothing is or can be hidden."
~ Ernest Holmes

We talked about chunking earlier and the importance of learning to think in various levels of abstraction. I firmly believe that the most abstract foundation of success is communication. If you are a master communicator, if you can excite, inspire, and motivate yourself and others, then your success is assured. Part three of this book has been dedicated, whether you were aware of it or not, to giving you some of the most powerful techniques available anywhere in the world to become a masterful communicator.

What is happening in your life right now is nothing more than a reflection of your Rule Book manifested in the world through your communication. Think about it for a second. You can't not communicate.

From the moment you were born, you are communicating all the time. Even as a baby, without language, you made yourself understood through a myriad of emotions, physical facial expressions, sounds, and body language.

Communication is the tool you use to navigate through life. The most successful people in history, regardless of your definition of success, have been masterful communicators. They have been able to inspire and motivate others, challenge paradigms and change the world.

WHAT ARE YOU COMMUNICATING?

Everything you do, don't do, say, or don't say is communicating something to the world around you. If you arrive late to a meeting, that action has communicated something about who you are, whether it's a fair assumption or not. If you are overweight, that visual representation communicates something about who you are, whether it's a fair assumption or not. If you smoke, that activity communicates something about who you are, whether it's a fair assumption or not.

The purpose here is not to judge what you choose to do, it is to make you see that *everything* you say and do is communicating something to the outside world about your character, your values, your intentions, and about what your boundaries are and what you are willing to accept in your life.

Once you understand that, you can make your own judgments about whether that is an accurate reflection of your character or not. Or make a choice that it may not be, and you wish to continue to do it anyway for whatever reason. Don't be fooled—communication is so much more than what you say.

One of the things that I have learned from my personal experience as well as from studying the most influential communicators of all time is the importance of character. In terms of creating long-term relationships, your character will eventually be communicated to the people with whom you interact through your consistent actions.

As Coach John Wooden of UCLA once said, "Be more concerned with your character than your reputation. Your reputation is merely who people think you are, your character is who you really are." It is therefore important to protect your character and guard your reputation. What you communicate to the world defines your character. This book is about providing you with the best information that will allow you to massively change your experience of the world and produce the results you truly want. How you use it will be depend on your character. Whether you are building a business, a nation, a family, or a relationship, the way you treat others and interact consistently with them will determine your long-term success.

This chapter is a round up of all the golden rules—things to remember as you start to change your world, perspectives that are helpful, that will assist you in creating win-win situations for you and your teammates.

YOUR MAP IS NOT THEIR TERRITORY EITHER

One of the keys to communication excellence is to understand that people's ideas of the world are different. Another person's "map" of the world is often referred to as their "model of the world;" the way they see and perceive things. Because people have different backgrounds, values, upbringings, and life experiences, they will have a model of the world that is entirely their own and unlike anybody else's. Dr. Milton Erickson said that someone's model of the world is as "unique as his or her thumbprint." Yet still we speak to each other and assume that what he is trying to convey and what is being interpreted are the same thing.

Communication is about respecting the individual and assisting them to understand what you are trying to say. In order to do that, you must learn to walk in their shoes and speak to them in their language.

A great example of this is written up in a study of Dr. Milton Erickson's work called *Phoenix* by David Gordon and Maribeth Meyers-Anderson. In this book, there is a case history of a six year-old boy who was sucking his thumb incessantly. His parents, who were both psychologists, tried everything they knew to get him to quit, but to no avail. Finally, they decided to bring him to see Dr. Milton Erickson the famous psychiatrist, and master communicator.

Dr. Milton Erickson sat in his office with the boy and his parents. He looked across at the young boy with his thumb in his mouth and then began to speak. "Your parents have brought you here so that I would get you to stop sucking your thumb." The boy looked defiantly at him, all the while continuing to suck his thumb.

"But, I don't have any right to tell you to stop it. Little six year-old boys have every right in the world to suck their thumbs, because that's what six year-old little boys do." The boy seemed to be pleased with this response as he looked victoriously at each of his parents while he continued to suck his thumb. Dr. Milton Erickson continued, "Of course a grown up seven year-old would never suck his thumb because a seven year-old is a young man. And a grown up seven year-old young man would never suck his thumb like a six year-old little boy."

The little boy stopped sucking his thumb a couple of months before his seventh birthday!

In this example, Dr. Erickson didn't attempt to use adult logic to change the little boy's behavior. Instead, he respected the child's model of the world and used it to assist him in wanting to change himself. In the little boy's model of the world, wanting to be a grown up seven year-old young man was important to him, so stopping the behavior was logical and obvious for him to do.

COMMUNICATION CAN ONLY BE DEEMED SUCCESSFUL WHEN YOU GET THE OUTCOME YOU DESIRE

Communication is a complex issue but essentially what you are creating in your reality right now is simply the result of your communication up to this point. If you are not getting the results that you want in your life, then chances are you are not communicating what you want to the world in a way that is understood. It is likely that your actions are communicating something very different than your words.

This is one reason why we went through the process of revealing your subconscious Rule Book earlier. Before you can communicate congruently with the Universe about what you want, you have to be aware of the filters that you are processing your reality through. For example, you could be frustrated that your employees have been spending excessively even after you have told them at meetings on several occasions that it was important to keep expenses down. You may assume that they're not listening to you because your words are not having the deterring effect on them you wanted. In fact, the extravagant company holiday party communicated loud and clear to them that money's not tight at all. It may be that one of your unconscious values is approval and the company party fulfilled that value, while that same value is in conflict with your value of being frugal. This misalignment in your values manifests itself in unclear communication, not to mention it also makes your company's success vulnerable to spending at a level you cannot actually afford. Your actions will reveal what is truly important to you, even if you aren't consciously aware of it yourself.

Until you can communicate congruently internally as well as externally about what you want you will always feel as though you are taking two steps forward and three steps back. What you say, how you behave, and what you do must all be in alignment with your dreams in order for them to become a reality.

TREAT PEOPLE AS YOU WOULD LIKE TO BE TREATED

We have all heard the biblical rule "Do unto others as you would have done unto you." It is without a doubt as relevant today as it was then. Sometimes in our haste to get through the day and get to our destination we forget that the people we are dealing with are just like us. They have their good days and bad days, they have their concerns and fears and deadlines just as we do. They would like to laugh and feel good about what they do just as we would.

As well as being one of the most important human relations principles of all time, it is also worth considering for the karmic effect of your actions. Whatever you dish out to the world will always come back around. Everything must be answered for and every debt must be cleared before we can learn the lessons that will allow us to evolve.

It is also jarring to remember that what you see tends to be a reflection of yourself. So if you see incompetence all around you, what does that say about you? If you see people doing the best they can with the resources they have, does that shift your perception and assist you in making the best choices?

DON'T MAKE A PRACTICE OF BURNING BRIDGES

I remember one day speaking with my friend Alejandro Ophilia, who was the former Chilean Ambassador to the United States and China. And Alejandro said, "One thing that I've learned in my life and my career is to never ever burn bridges."

Some of my most important lessons in life have come from difficult situations with other people. It is easy to be around people we like, but often there is as much, if not more, to be gained in understanding our own behaviors and beliefs by being around people we don't particularly like. If nothing else, it serves as a reminder of who we don't want to become.

I once knew a woman who controlled her environment perfectly. She didn't have people around who didn't agree with her or challenge her or in any way rock her boat. That way she was okay. If any of her friends did challenge her, they were kicked out of the group. Each time she would burn that bridge completely and there would be no reconciliation.

It worked from the standpoint of controlling what was in her immediate environment, but what she didn't realize was that there was a price to pay for this type of behavior. Her reputation suffered. People didn't want to work with her. People didn't want to create long-term relationships with her.

As a result, she began to feel badly about the way she treated others and grew lonely and sad. In addition, she missed business opportunities to deepen relationships, was not given referrals, and couldn't continue to broaden her financial horizons. When you only keep people around who agree with you, you aren't challenged, therefore you don't grow. Any vision or business that is not growing is stagnating, and will eventually end.

Not only do you never know where that person will resurface in your future, but you don't want someone damaging your reputation. So it is always best to leave everything on amicable ground. Be the sort of person that people bump into five years later and are genuinely excited and happy to see again.

INTEGRITY – BE TRUTHFUL AND HONEST

"To be persuasive, we must be believable.
To be believable, we must be credible.
To be credible, we must be truthful."
~ Edward R. Murrow

Integrity is about adhering to a code of conduct. It is the difference between right and wrong and sticking to that code no matter what. It's all very easy to stick to your principles when there is no pressure to do so, but what has marked out the outstanding men and women of history is that they have shown strength and determination in the face of opposition. Take Rosa Parks, for example. Her personal belief and ethics about right and wrong were so strong that she personally opposed segregation and as a result went down in history as a major force for change.

When Jesus of Nazareth invited prostitutes, tax collectors and the poor to eat with him he was demonstrating his integrity and beliefs in a way far more powerful than words alone could ever do. Despite being looked down upon by the church and the other religious leaders of the time, it communicated a very powerful message of inclusion and the love and acceptance of God for all. It was also a message of loving one's neighbor and non-judgment. It was a message of walking one's talk with congruency.

Don't, however, confuse honesty and integrity with the need to reveal all information. In *The Philosopher's Stone*, Harry Potter's first adventure, toward the end of his journey after he has defeated the Dark Lord, he asks Professor Dumbledore about his past and his parents, "Sir, there are some things I'd like to know, if you can tell me... things I want to know the truth about..." "The truth," Dumbledore sighed, "It is a beautiful and terrible thing, and should therefore be treated with great caution."

I happen to agree with him for a number of reasons. The first is that there is to some extent no such thing as "the" truth. There is only "a" truth. Secondly, there is such a thing as "too much information." Why, for example, tell a client that you were up all night fixing a mistake that you made in preparation? It's the truth but it doesn't help anyone. All it does is create doubt in your ability to do the job.

It's important in communicating your intentions to the world to sometimes hide your cards and keep a poker face. There have been times in my life when I felt the need to discuss all of my intentions with every one. Honesty and integrity are two of my highest values, and I used to have a belief that to be absolutely honest, I would have to wear my intentions on my sleeve. The problem with that type of thinking is that often in life it can produce results that are not very satisfying.

Often revealing intentions is detrimental to the end result. In a poker game, you would never show your hand to the other players. However, sometimes when we feel that we are not in a strong position, we want to show the world our strength and have a desire to reveal it to others in order to build ourselves up. I had a client call me not too long ago and he was upset. He had set several goals in his business that he knew would stretch him. He considered the goals to be quite lofty, but he was resolved to make them happen.

The reason he was upset was that his family didn't take him seriously, because he had let them down on a few occasions in the past. In an attempt to build himself up in their eyes, he told several of them about his new goals he had set. When he told them, they did not react enthusiastically. In fact, they attempted to, in his words, "beat him down" and convince him that he wasn't being realistic. After I talked with him for awhile, I finally asked him, "How would your family members have felt if you had never said anything, but instead had simply come through with the results?" "They would be very happy," he replied. "And, how would you feel if you had never said anything but had just shown up one day having produced the results?" "Ecstatic," he replied.

His family wasn't attempting to hurt him; they were simply acting the only way they could based upon their model of the world. They were doing the best they could with the resources they had available at the time. My client wanted to gain their respect by telling them what he had planned. This actually did just the opposite. The illusion was that he would get acceptance or power by revealing his intentions, when in fact it actually took them away. Moreover, if he did produce the result afterward, he would be proving them wrong and they might take less joy in his accomplishment. Often the best thing to do is to keep your hand to yourself like a master card player until the right moment is revealed to reveal your royal straight flush!

DON'T TALK ABOUT "I"

They say the sweetest sound in any language is the sound of your own name. When communicating with others, you will find that most people are interested in themselves more then anything else. One effective way to increase your influence and effectiveness in communication is to stop speaking about yourself but instead engage the other person in discussion about themselves. Also remember, in his 2000 State of the Union Address President Bill Clinton used the word "we" 208 times. This single small word goes a long way in establishing a strong team spirit.

NEVER SPEAK POORLY OF OTHERS

Speaking poorly of others is a sure fire way to ruin your reputation. I worked with a man who spoke about everybody within the company behind their backs. He thought that he was gaining people's trust by confiding in them. What it actually did was show people that he couldn't be trusted and that he was liable to speak poorly about them when they were not around. It also creates ill will and a lack of respect within a team, group, or organization.

One of my good friends, Jim, told me a story about an occasion when he was out to lunch with a perspective business associate. The woman he was having lunch with had had a few drinks and was beginning to get quite talkative. At one point in the luncheon she overheard someone at a table next to them who had mentioned the name of someone who was a competitor in her line of work. When she overheard the name, she turned to the person who had mentioned it and said "Oh, I know Mike!" The person sitting next to them asked, "How do you know Mike?" As they spoke, this woman revealed her oopion that "He's only out for himself and he rips people off all the time." "Oh really," the other guy said, "What's your name?" She told him and then he said, "Well, he's a good friend of mine. I'll let him know you feel that way."

It does us absolutely no good whatsoever to voice opinions like that, even if we believe they're true. It effects and tarnishes our reputations more then it does the person we are speaking of.

YOU CAN'T PLEASE ALL OF THE PEOPLE ALL OF THE TIME

> *"You can please some of the people all of the time and all of the people some of the time but you can't please all of the people all of the time."*
>
> ~ Winston Churchill

The one trait that runs consistent with almost every influential person I have ever researched or met is that they took a stand for what they believed in no matter the consequences. They put their ideas or concepts out to the world despite the abuse or criticism that resulted. The moment you take a stand for anything, you will also encounter those in your world who oppose your position.

As Einstein once said, "Great spirits have always encountered violent opposition from mediocre minds."

When Gandhi stood for the freedom of the Indian people, he was beaten down and thrown in jail by the British. When Nelson Mandela stood for the equality of the blacks in Africa, he was thrown in jail for a good portion of his life.

But they won and their contribution to the world has gone down in history. And who knows, yours may too!

NINETEEN

Conclusion:
The One Thing That
Can Change Everything

*"The measure of a man's real character is what he would do
if he knew he never would be found out."*
~ Thomas B. Macaulay

One thing can change everything. One event, one thought, one act of kindness, one act of violence, one moment can change everything. This book could be your one thing.

We are each given our own individual Universe to shape as we will. We are constantly shaping our Universe all the time, either consciously or unconsciously. Every thought we have, every word we utter, every action we take communicates something to the Universe around us and sculpts it in some way. By practicing and learning the skills taught in this book you empower yourself to take conscious control of the tools that define your world each and every moment of your life. This book is not meant to be read one time through, but rather to be a reference and guidebook to be revisited over and over again.

Remember that you now have the power to strategically see, hear, feel and create your future then literally carve it out in the way you choose. You now have the power and knowledge to win the "Game of Life."

In life, the people who are able to produce the most in terms of results are those who have the ability to enlist the cooperation of others to assist them in accomplishing their objectives. By mastering your interpersonal communication skills as well as your ability to influence, you are empowered to produce extraordinary results.

You have the capacity to master all that is contained in this book. You have the power to change the Game you play and to control the size of the Game you play.

Use the tools contained in this book to expand your Rule Book and reach outward with new strategies and skill sets to gain understanding in new areas. Break through the boundary conditions of your current thinking to embrace ALL that is possible for you! By doing that you will forge opportunities you never thought possible and the Playing Field of your Game will expand.

ALL THAT IS POSSIBLE   YOU

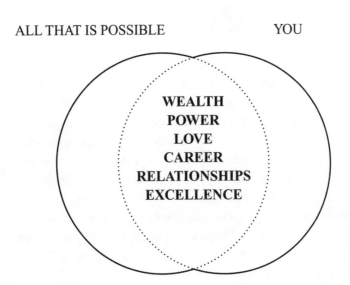

WEALTH
POWER
LOVE
CAREER
RELATIONSHIPS
EXCELLENCE

Most of all, learn to believe in yourself and your ability to create a magical reality. Because reality is only what you choose it to be.

Always remember to use the tools and skills with your heart and with caring for your brothers and sisters on the planet. Truly, if there is nothing outside of you and we are all one, then the Golden Rule becomes "Do unto yourself as you would have done unto you." If people really understood that we are all one, than the world would be a very different place. We would not harm others or our planet but instead live peacefully, respecting our differences, and caring for our natural resources.

When I was growing up, my grandparents had a small place on the beach near Ensenada, Mexico that was always vacant, and family and friends were welcome to stay there when they were in the area. My grandparents had only one request, and that was that everyone who stayed there leave the place a little nicer than it was before they came. As you take these skills and go on your way to wealth, power, and influencing your world in positive ways, I have only one request, and that is that you leave the world a little nicer then it was before you came. I hope to meet you at some point in the future. Until then, take care, dream big dreams, and make each day an extraordinary adventure.

APPENDIX
The Quantum Facts

The "path" comes into existence only when we observe it.
~ Werner Heisenberg, *Uncertainty Principle*

In 1927, physicist Werner Heisenberg set the cat amongst the pigeons by publishing what has come to be known as the *Uncertainty Principle*. It had profound implications and started a debate about the very nature of reality that would rage the better part of 55 years.

Up until the time that science started to explore the quantum nature of the Universe, it was popular to believe that the Universe followed the laws of Newtonian Physics—that a "real world" existed independently of us, regardless of what we did in it. What Heisenberg's conclusive study on particle behavior did was blow that assumption apart. This had far-reaching implications from both a scientific and philosophical point of view.

Heisenberg's theory states quite simply that "the more precisely the *position* is determined, the less precisely the *momentum* is known." Translated into "classic physics," this meant that, contrary to popular belief, the future motion of a particle *could not* be exactly predicted, or "determined" from a knowledge of its present position and momentum and all of the forces acting upon it.

In brief, Heisenberg's *Uncertainty Principle* implied that there was no concrete reality! Rather, reality depended on who or what was observing it.

Indeed in quantum research, when scientists set up an experiment expecting light to behave as a wave, it behaved as a wave; when they presupposed it as a particle, it behaved as a

271

particle. Many experiments in quantum physics have also told us that a quantum particle only exists as a possibility prior to our observing or measuring it; this means that *it doesn't exist until we look for it to exist.*

As you can imagine, in 1927, that was a pretty radical concept (and it still is today!) The heavyweights of the time came out against it, Einstein being one of them. Einstein was perplexed that the simple act of observation could actually affect the object of observation. He did not believe that an observer could bring about drastic changes in the Universe simply by looking at it.

Einstein believed that Heisenberg's interpretation of quantum mechanics was incomplete. So Einstein and a few buddies —Podoski and Rosen—set out to disprove Heisenberg's *Uncertainty Principle* in a thought experiment in 1935, known as the *E.P.R. Paradox.*

In this thought experiment, these three leading quantum theorists postulated that one *could* know the position and momentum (or spin) of a quantum particle simultaneously...by sending two electrons out in separate directions from a single source pulse at the same speed and measuring the position of one and momentum of the other. Both position and momentum of each could be accurately predicted.

This led to a huge debate between Einstein and Niels Bohr, another leading quantum theorist who favored Heisenberg's ideas. Niels Bohr stated that Einstein's E.P.R. theory was based on the faulty assumption that observing the position of one didn't somehow affect the momentum of the other. Einstein claimed that it would be impossible for the observation of one electron to affect the other because that would mean that the electrons would have to communicate in some way across the quanta. And for that to occur, "communication" would have taken place at over seven times the speed of light, or instantaneously, which according to the theory of relativity was impossible. According to Einstein, nothing can move faster than the speed of light.

It wasn't until 1982, that the Einstein/Bohr debate was finally answered. In a laboratory at the University of Paris a research team led by physicist Alain Aspect performed a series of experiments based upon a mathematical theorem that was put forward by John Bell in 1964, to settle the Einstein/Bohr debate. These experiments may turn out to be the most important experiments of the 20th century.

What has come to be known as the Aspect Experiment revealed something remarkable—that under certain circumstances, subatomic particles such as electrons are able to communicate with each other regardless of distance. This communication happened instantaneously whether they were separated by a fraction of a millimeter or a hundred miles. According to Einstein, it wasn't possible because it meant that the communication traveled faster than anything, which at the time was considered impossible. Aspect, however, in 1982, proved once and for all that not only did they communicate but they did so instantaneously—what one particle "knew" they all "knew" at the same time.

The Aspect experiment implied that there is an underlying connectedness to everything in the Universe. However, this same experiment proved something else as well. It proved what Heisenberg had stated in his *Uncertainty Principle*, that *in a quantum reality, the observer always and intimately affects the observed.* In fact, you can't observe something *without* affecting it.

And here's where it starts to get really interesting...

In the University of London, physicist David Bohm took Aspect's findings one step further and suggested that objective "reality" does not exist at all and that despite an apparent solidity, the Universe is essentially an illusion—a gigantic, intricately detailed, and complex holographic illusion.

To understand why Bohm makes such a startling assertion, it is important to explain what a hologram is.

A hologram is a three-dimensional image made with the aid of a laser. If you are a Star Trek fan you will be aware of holograms and the holodeck (which as we will see may be closer to reality than we would have ever thought possible.) Or perhaps you saw them used in *Star Wars* when R2D2 projects a 3-D image of Princess Leah bearing a message from Obi-Wan Kenobi.

To make a hologram, the object is first cast in the light of a laser beam. Then a second laser beam is bounced off the reflected light of the first. The point where they meet is captured on film. When the film is developed it looks like a meaningless swirl of light and dark lines. But as soon as the developed film is illuminated by another laser beam, a three-dimensional image of the original object appears.

What is so fascinating is that if you create a hologram of an apple and then you cut the holographic image in half—or for that matter into a thousand pieces—each piece will contain the whole image of the apple, just a smaller but complete version of it. Each part of a hologram therefore contains all the information possessed by the whole. The "whole is in every part." This could then explain why communication between particles is instantaneous—the Universe is holographic in nature, and therefore everything in it is a part of the whole. The particles are not necessarily communicating but rather their separateness is just an illusion. They are part of the whole, and the whole is in the part. Bohm argues that at some deeper level of reality such particles are not individual entities, but are actually extensions of the same fundamental whole—whatever that is!

To enable people to better understand this idea, Bohm offers the following example. Imagine there is an aquarium. You are watching all the "action" by way of closed circuit TV. There are two screens relating to two cameras trained on the aquarium from two difference angles. As you watch the two screens you might assume that you are actually watching two different aquariums. You continue to watch and start to notice that when one fish moves the fish in the "other tank" makes a corresponding change. Amazing you think—these fish must be "talking" to each other.

This, says Bohm, is precisely what is going on between the subatomic particles in Aspect's experiment. According to Bohm, the apparent faster-than-light connection is really telling us that there is some deeper level of reality we are not privy to, a more complex dimension. Like in the aquarium example where there were not two fish at all—just one fish from a different perspective. We were simply not able to see the full picture to be able to work that out.

In addition to the mind bending qualities you may currently be experiencing, such a holographic Universe would possess other amazing features. If the separateness is an illusion it means that at some level that we do not yet understand that we are all interconnected. We are all just swimming in a quantum ocean of pure potentiality. Modern science is now restating what the ancient traditions have always held to be true—that you are one with everything in the Universe. Everything is one energy manifesting in almost infinite diversity. As scientists began to study more and more minute levels of matter, they began to see that at the smallest levels—smaller than the atom—there is more space than there is solidity. In fact, if you examined this book, or yourself for that matter, under a high-powered microscope you would see more space than you would solid matter. According to quantum field theorists, the atoms of which the book is made are 99.999 percent composed of the void and emptiness of space. The subatomic particles are impulses of energy and information. What gives the appearance of matter is the arrangement and quantity of the subatomic particles. The density of the arrangement and the vibratory rate determine the form that something takes in the material world.

So a BMW, a pitbull terrier, you, the Grand Canyon, Niagara Falls, and The Sydney Opera House—everything in the world right now is made up of exactly the same "stuff." Look around you right now. Everything you can see and touch is the same matter—every person, every object, and every star in the sky. The only thing that is different about each thing is their density and vibrational frequency.

Bohm is not the only researcher who has found evidence that the Universe is a hologram. Working independently in the field of brain research, Stanford neurophysiologist Karl Pribram has also realized the holographic nature of reality.

Pribram was drawn to the holographic model by the puzzle of how and where memories are stored in the brain. For decades, numerous studies have shown that rather than being confined to a specific location, memories are dispersed throughout the brain.

Beginning in the 1913, Canadian Neurosurgeon Wilder Penfield did several experiments in which he probed his patients' brains with an electrode in an attempt to cure their epilepsy. In the 1930's, he made some astounding discoveries. In one such case, he found while studying a female patient that when he touched certain areas of her brain, she recalled a vivid memory of being in her kitchen and hearing the sounds of her little boy playing outside. She could also hear the sounds of the passing automobiles and other neighborhood noises.

What Penfield had actually discovered was that the stimulation of a certain portion of the cerebral cortex could evoke incredibly vivid memories. Penfield's research led many scientists at the time to believe that *memory* was stored *in* the brain. This belief about the storage of memory was widely held in the scientific community for many years, although it remained impossible to find the *individual* locations of *specific* memories.

In a series of landmark experiments in the 1920's, brain scientist Karl Lashley found that no matter what portion of a rat's brain he removed, the rat was still able to run a complex maze it had been taught prior to surgery. In fact, when the rat was left with nothing but a brain stem it was still able to run the maze.

It was in the late 1950's that Karl Pribram, a leading neurophysiologist from Stanford University, took up the case and proposed his groundbreaking theory for the *holographic* storage of memory. He explained that in Karl Lashley's experiments it was possible for the rats to continue to run the maze even without much of a brain, because the memory was not in a specific location in the brain, but rather it was stored holographically throughout the entire brain.

Pribram believes memories are encoded not in neurons or small groupings of neurons, but in patterns of nerve impulses that crisscross the entire brain in the same way that patterns of laser light crisscross the entire area of a piece of film containing a holographic image. In other words, Pribram believes the brain itself is a hologram.

Pribram's theory also explains how the human brain can store so many memories in so little space. It has been estimated that the human brain has the capacity to memorize something on the order of 10 billion bits of information during the average human lifetime (or roughly the same amount of information contained in five sets of the Encyclopaedia Britannica).

The storage of memory is not the only neurophysiological puzzle that becomes more feasible in light of Pribram's holographic model of the brain. Another is how the brain is able to translate the avalanche of frequencies it receives via the senses into the concrete world of our perceptions. Encoding and decoding frequencies is precisely what a hologram does best. Pribram concludes, just as a hologram functions as a sort of lens—a translating device able to convert an apparently meaningless blur of frequencies into a coherent image—the brain also comprises a lens and uses holographic principles to convert the frequencies it receives through the senses into "hard" reality.

But the most mind-boggling aspect of Pribram's holographic model of the brain is what happens when it is put together with Bohm's theory. For if the concreteness of the world is but a secondary reality and what is "there" is actually a holographic blur of frequencies, and if the brain is also a hologram and only selects some of the frequencies out of this blur and transforms them into sensory perceptions, what becomes of objective reality?

Put quite simply, it ceases to exist. As the religions of the East have long upheld, the material world is Maya, an illusion, and although we may think we are physical beings moving through a physical world, this too is an illusion.

We are really "receivers" floating through a kaleidoscopic sea of frequency, and what we extract from this sea and interpret into physical reality is but one view taken from an infinite sea of possibility. The implications of this perspective are enormous.

Just think about it for a second. If "reality" is different for everyone because everyone translates frequency differently, and therefore everyone chooses a different experience from a sea of possibility, doesn't it then follow that if you can understand more about the way you translate the frequency you then have the power to change your world? So if you don't particularly enjoy your current reality you have the opportunity to shift-focus to an alternative reality from the sea of possibility.

The implications are indeed profound. If it is all just a hologram with an infinite number of possible "channels" to choose from, and all we need to do is tune in to whatever we choose to experience, then there truly are no limits to the extent you can alter the fabric and outcomes of your life.

All things exist in this quantum soup of pure potentiality. Your external reality is nothing but a blank canvas waiting for you to choose your channel and create your masterpiece...

ABOUT THE AUTHOR

Christopher Howard
Author, Leadership Advisor, and Results Coach

Christopher Howard is one of the world's leading authorities on accelerated human change and personal achievement. He is an entrepreneur who has personally led, managed, launched, and turned around numerous organizations and businesses. As CEO of The Christopher Howard Companies, he captivates audiences internationally each year through his public seminars and media appearances, assisting hundreds of thousands of people to unleash their potential and live their dreams. Howard's clients include politicians, Fortune 500 executives, celebrities, and thousands of people from all walks of life who want to improve their finances, health, relationships, and careers. Because of his dynamic presence and unique approach to achieving success, Christopher Howard has been featured on numerous television and radio programs worldwide.

AN INTRODUCTION TO
THE CHRISTOPHER HOWARD COMPANIES
by Chris Howard

We all have dreams and desires for our lives. Why is it that sometimes we get what we want and sometimes we don't? Why do we start out in the direction of our goals only to find ourselves off course or falling short of what we know we are capable of? And more importantly, how can we consistently accomplish the goals we set for ourselves to live the life of our dreams?

Those were some of the questions I began asking myself at a time in my life when I was $70,000 in debt, living in someone else's garage apartment, and feeling I had few prospects for my future. I had already taken countless seminars and read all the best-sellers on personal development, so I knew what to do, just not how to do it. It was when I started to write down my goals and take personal responsibility to shift my focus toward what I truly desired that everything in my thinking and my life started to shift. Instead of dwelling on the feeling that I was not where I wanted to be, I asked myself, what is the difference between those people who have wealth and riches beyond their wildest dreams and those who live from paycheck to paycheck? Because the mind always seeks resolution, that one unanswered question sent me on a quest studying the lives of great leaders in every field and caused me to develop my system of Speed Modeling™ that eventually resulted in the growth of The Christopher Howard Companies.

The answer to that question—what sets successful leaders apart—is their mindsets, focus, strategies, behaviors, beliefs, values, and many other internal factors that determine our experiences in life. The Christopher Howard Companies were established to give individuals and organizations those particular skills, attitudes, and mindsets to turn their boldest visions and intentions into realities. Most people go through life believing they have to cope with themselves as they are and deal with life as it comes because, "that's just the way it is." The scientific fact is, reality is subjective, therefore, you can actually create your life however you want it. You can forever transform aspects of your personality that no longer serve you and manifest your deepest heart's desires. I developed Creation Technologies™ as a specific set of tools that literally re-pattern thinking on a neurological level to replicate the thinking and behavioral patterns of success.

I am not interested in pumping people up over the course of a weekend only to have them go home and have their lives gradually return to "normal," as is so many people's experience with seminars. Our trainings and programs are unique in that participants not only undergo a profound change on both a conscious and subconscious level, they also take with them specific techniques to apply in their daily lives to remain focused and motivated through the accomplishment of their intended goals. If you are ready to finally take charge of your reality and live the life you know you are meant to live, these are the two paths to success that will absolutely assist you in getting from here to there.

UNIVERSITY OF EXCELLENCE

Breakthrough to Success – Wealth and Power Weekend

It's within this course that you are introduced to the latest cutting-edge technologies to take charge of your thinking, and therefore, your results. If it's now time to experience ultimate wealth, optimal health, and fulfilling relationships, begin here. During this two-and-a-half-day event, you finally release those limiting beliefs that have been holding you back from the accomplishment of your greatest intentions, then you navigate your future with Strategic Visioning™ to propel you toward your dreams with more momentum and ease than you ever knew possible.

Performance Revolution

Here is applied the most powerful techniques of Creation Technologies™ and Neuro Linguistics to the business environment. This powerful and exciting weekend gives you the success strategies and insights extracted from billionaires and other legends of the business world that will take your finances, communication, and leadership skills to a whole new level. These new skills will ultimately set you apart from the competition and give you the edge you need to powerfully move forward. Whatever your career goals, Performance Revolution will provide you with the recipe for success!

Design Your Destiny

Do you ever find yourself wondering, "What is my purpose in life? What path can I take to get there?" Many people carry this aching feeling around with them, a sense that they are not fulfilling their destiny or contributing to the world in the way they sense they can. This three-and-a-half-day experience called Design Your Destiny will help you remember your true vision, mission, and purpose, then access the power within yourself to make it real. You will get clear on exactly what you intend for your life, plot your course, then begin to take powerful steps to drive you forward toward your ultimate vision and destiny.

Leadership Explosion

Imagine if you could sit down with some of the world's most powerful leaders, like Nelson Mandela, Bill Gates, or Oprah Winfrey, and learn the secrets of what made their achievements inevitable, and then install their mindsets in yourself to fulfill your own dreams. Leadership Explosion transforms your life instantly and forever with an in-depth modeling project and hypnotic processes that install excellence within you. You walk away from this one-week intensive possessing a new level of leadership abilities and personal power, the very qualities you admire in others. This week-long training will enable you to lead others toward the success of your own grand vision.

LEADERSHIP AND COACHING ACADEMY

If you're ready to learn the techniques of Creation Technologies™ and Neuro Linguistics to lead, coach, or empower yourself and others, join us for professional certification training at our Leadership and Coaching Academy.

Breakthrough to Success – Wealth and Power Weekend

This serves as the basis to begin this Leadership and Coaching path. It is the best platform from which to launch a new career, master powerful communication, and even develop your own skills as a trainer.

Results Coach Certification

This one-week training gives you the necessary skills modeled from masters of communication and accelerated human transformation to coach and lead others to produce exceptional results. You will learn how to harness the power of the other 90% of your mind—your unconscious – using the techniques of Creation Technologies™, Neuro Linguistics, and Neurological Repatterning™. With the set of skills learned at this level, you can empower your clients, colleagues, family, and self to breakthrough behavioral patterns and achieve results in finances, health, relationships, and career.

Master Results Coach and Performance Consultant Certification

This next level of coaching and leadership training goes deeper into uncovering the personal Values, Attitudes, Meta Programs, which are thinking patterns, and the Internal Filters that determine exactly what we get in life. With an understanding of how you create your reality and a range of techniques using Neurological Repatterning™ and Quantum Linguistics, you can consult, teach, and empower people in business and organizations to make long-lasting changes in their mind-body connection and permanently stop unwanted behaviors.

Platform Skills and Trainer's Training

In this one-week training, you install 36 behaviors of the most effective speakers at the unconscious level so that you are able to persuade and inspire groups of people. Use the power of language and rapport to create synergistic relationships and expand your personal and professional sphere of influence.

Master Trainers Development

After completing all levels of the Leadership and Coaching Academy, you have the ability to assist at every level of The Christopher Howard Companies' on-going trainings. Our staff of Master Results Coaches and trainers also provides any ongoing support you need as you successfully incorporate all your new skills into your own personal and professional development.

AVAILABLE PRODUCTS

BOOK
Three Steps to Wealth and Power: Unleash Your Potential for Unlimited Achievement

Three Steps to Wealth and Power is the result of my studying those individuals who have achieved greatness and made a profound impact on the world as a result. If you are ready to finally tap into the unlimited abundance you deserve, or you want to influence those around you toward the achievement of your life's mission, this book will accelerate that process.

CD SETS
Performance Revolution

Within leadership lies the power of influence. Your success can be instantly and exponentially increased by developing your leadership abilities. From this explosive 8-CD set, you can learn the business strategies that will multiply your returns, including how to create a team, negotiate win-wins, and consistently arrive at the outcomes you set for yourself.

Stepping Into Wealth

Shifting your focus can instantly transform your financial destiny. Discover what you really believe about what is possible for you, then learn how to replace those limiting beliefs with ones that will propel you toward real prosperity. This 3-CD program includes a powerful hypnotic induction that you can play over and over again to install the mindset of abundance at ever deeper levels.

Skyrocket Your Sales

This 2-CD program teaches you how to use hypnotic language to increase your sales ability. Learn the fastest and most successful way to close a deal, generate relationships with your prospects, and respond to major objections with "sleight of mouth" patterns. This CD set also includes a hypnotic induction that will cause you to achieve your specific, pre-set financial goals.

The 7 Keys to Wealth

Are you ready to finally achieve mastery with money? From modeling legendary financial giants from multi-billionaires Warren Buffett to Richard Branson, you learn seven behaviors and beliefs that consistently generate wealth. In this exciting new 2-CD program you can upgrade the software of your own mind with more effective habits to align with your business goals and cause you to prosper. Take a closer look at your own misconceptions about money and learn the masters' secrets that can launch you toward tremendous riches.

VIDEO
Soar to Success

Discover four major principles of Creation Technologies™ that form the foundation for achieving consistent results in life. These Four Lessons in Success can catapult you to a new way of thinking that will ensure your long-term health and wealth, including the power of focus and taking effective action toward your goals.

Bibliography

A&E Home Video, *Martin Luther King Jr., The Man and the Dream*, New Video Group, New York, NY, 1997

Ansari, Masud, Ph.D., **Modern Hypnosis**, Mas-Press, Washington, D.C., 1982

Arabian Knights, Babelsberg International Film Produktion, Hallmark Entertainment, 1999

Branson, Richard, **Losing My Virginity: Richard Branson The Autobiography**, Random House, Australia, 1999

Bandler, Richard., and La Valle, John. **Persuasion Engineering**, Meta Publications, Inc., Capitola, CA, 1996

Beckwith, Michael, Ph.D., **40 Day Mind Fast Soul Feast**, Agape Publishing, Inc., Culver City, CA, 2000

Bower, Tom, **Branson**, Harper Collins, UK, 2000

Brown, Mick, **Richard Branson: The Authorised Biography**, Headline Book Publishing, UK, 1988

Buffet, Mary and Clark, David, **The New Buffetology**, Simon & Schuster Ltd., UK, 2002

Buffett, Warren and Cunningham, Lawrence A., **The Essays of Warren Buffett: Lessons for Corporate America**, Library of Congress Cataloging-in-Publication Data, 1997

Buzan, Tony with Barry Buzan, **The Mind Map Book: How to Use Radiant Thinking to Maximize Your Brain's Untapped Potential**, Penguin Books, New York, NY, 1993

Carnegie, Dale, **Lifetime Plan for Success**, Galahad Books, New York, NY, 1998

Carroll, Lewis. **Alice in Wonderland**, W.W. Norton & Company, New York, NY, 1971

Chopra, Deepak, M.D., **Ageless Body, Timeless Mind**, Harmony Books, New York, NY, 1993

Chopra, Deepak M.D., **Creating Affluence: Wealth Consciousness in the Field of All Possibilities**, New World Library, San Rafael, CA, 1993

Chopra, Deepak, M.D. **Quantum Healing**, Bantam Books, New York, NY, 1989

289

Cialdini, Robert B., **Influence: The Psychology of Persuasion**, Quill, New York, NY, 1984

Csikszentmihalyi, Mihaly, **Flow: The Psychology of Optimal Experience**, Harper & Row Publishers, New York, NY, 1990

Dearlove, Des, **Business the Richard Branson Way: 10 Secrets of the World's Greatest Brand Builder**, AMACOM, New York, NY, 1999

Dilts, Robert, **Sleight of Mouth**, Meta Publications, Capitola, CA, 1999

Fridson, Martin S., **How To Be A Billionaire: Proven Strategies From the Titans of Wealth**, John Wiley & Sons, Inc., New York, NY, 2000

Gaines, Charles, *Men's Health Magazine*, "Staying Hungry," Wenner Media, New York, NY, 2004

Gleick, James, **Chaos: Making a New Science**, Viking Press, New York, NY, 1987

Goodwin, Paul A., Ph.D., *Foundation Theory: Report on the Efficacy of the Formal Education Process in Rural Alaska*, Volume I. Advanced Neuro Dynamics, Honolulu, HI, 1988

Gordon, David and Meyers-Anderson, Maribeth, **Phoenix**, Meta Publications, Capitola, CA, 1981

Graham, Benjamin, **The Intelligent Investor: The Definitive Book of Value Investing**, HarperCollins, New York, NY, 1984

Greene, Robert, **The 48 Laws of Power**, Viking Penguin, New York, NY, 1998

Griffith, Joe., **Speaker's Library of Business Quotations**, Prentice Hall, Inc., Englewood Cliffs, N J, 1990

Hart, Michael H., **The 100: A Ranking of the Most Influential Persons in History**, Hart Pub. Co., New York, NY, 1978

Hawking, Stephen, **The Universe in a Nutshell**, Bantam Books, New York, NY, 2001

Jackson, Tim, **Virgin King: Inside Richard Branson's Business Empire**, HarperCollins, UK, 1994

Jung, Carl, **Psychological Types**, Princeton University Press, Princeton, NJ, 1971

Karrass, Chester L., **The Negotiating Game**, Harper Business, New York, NY, 1992

Karrass, Chester L., **In Business as in Life—You Don't Get What You Deserve, You Get What You Negotiate**, Stanford St. Press, Beverly Hills, CA, 1996

Katherine, Anne, M.A. **Boundaries**, Parkside Publishing Corporation, New York, NY, 1991

Knight, Sue, **NLP at Work: The Difference that Makes a Difference in Business**, Nicholas Brealey Publishing, London, 1995

Korzybski, Alfred, **Science and Sanity: An Introduction to Non-Aristotelian Systems and General Semantics**, Institute of General Semantics, Brooklyn, NY, 1995

Krasner, A.M., Ph.D., **The Wizard Within**, American Board of Hypnotherapy Press Irvine, CA, 1990, 1991

Jung, Carl G., **Man and his Symbols**, Doubleday & Company Inc., New York, NY, 1964

Laborde, Genie Z., **Influencing with Integrity: Management Skills for Communication and Negotiation**, Syntony Publishing, Palo Alta, CA, 1983

Lowe, Janet, **Warren Buffett Speaks: Wit and Wisdom from the World's Greatest Investor**, John Wiley & Sons, Inc., New York, NY, 1997

Lowe, Janet, **Ted Turner Speaks: Insights From the World's Greatest Maverick**, John Wiley & Sons, Inc., New York, NY, 1999

Lowenstein, Roger, **Buffet: The Making of an American Capitalist**, Doubleday, New York, NY, 1995

Massey, Morris, **The People Puzzle**, Reston Publishing Company, Reston, VA, Inc., 1979

Myss, Caroline, Ph.D., **Anatomy of the Spirit**, Three Rivers Press, New York, NY, 1996

PBS Home Video, *The Long Walk of Nelson Mandela*, UnaPix Entertainment, Inc. and WGBH/Frontline, 1999

Ponder, Catherine, **The Dynamic Laws of Prosperity**, DeVorss & Company, Marina del Rey, CA, 1962

Penfield, Wilder, **The Mystery of the Mind: A Critical Study of Consciousness and the Human Brain**, Princeton University Press, Princeton, N.J., 1975

Peters, Thomas J.; and Waterman Jr., Robert H., **In Search of Excellence**, Harper & Row Publishers, New York, NY, 1982

Ries, Al. and Trout, Jack, **Positioning**, Warner Books, New York, NY, 1981

Robbins, Anthony, **Unlimited Power**, Simon and Schuster, New York, NY, 1986

Rohm, Wendy Goldman, **The Murdoch Mission**, John Wiley & Sons, Inc., Library of Congress Cataloging-in-Publication Data, New York, NY, 2002

Rohmann, Chris, **A World of Ideas**, Ballantine Publishing Group, New York, NY,1999

Satir, Virginia, **The New Peoplemaking,** Science and Behavior Books, Inc., Mountain View, CA,1988

Sharp, Daryl, **C.G. Jung Lexicon**, Inner City Books, Toronto, Canada, 1991

Shawcross, William, **Murdoch: The Making of a Media Empire**, Simon & Schuster Touchstone, New York, NY, 2002

Soundworks, International, Inc., The *Greatest Speeches of All Time*, The Nostalgia Company, Rolling Bay, WA, 1998

Talbot, Michael, **The Holographic Universe**, HarperCollins, New York, NY, 1991

Trump, Donald J. with Schwartz, Tony, **Trump: The Art of the Deal**, Warner Books, New York, NY, 1987

The Great Outdoors, Universal Studios, Los Angeles, CA, 1988

Walsch, Neale Donald, **The Little Soul and the Sun**, Hampton Roads Publishing Company, Inc., Charlottesville, VA, 1998

Wolf, Fred Alan, **Taking the Quantum Leap**, Harper and Row Publishers, Inc., New York, NY, 1981

Index

A

Abstract/Specific 58, 97, 126, 216
Attitudes 48, 61, 90, 125, 285

B

Bandler, Richard 289
Beliefs 47, 61, 88, 124
Brain 45, 291
Branson, Richard 12, 27-28, 85-86, 88-90, 94, 98-99, 101-102, 124,
131-133, 161, 239, 251- 253, 288-290
Buffett, Warren 17, 51, 85, 88, 90, 92-94, 96, 98-100, 103, 112, 133,
243, 289-289, 291

C

Challenge Response 59, 98, 126
Chunking 213-216
Commitment 228
Communication 217, 255, 257-258, 291
Comparison 59, 98, 126
Consistency 228
Convincer 54, 93, 126
Creation Technologies™ 8-11, 27-28, 38, 50, 128, 282-285, 288

D

Decisions 49, 61, 89, 126
Deletion 42
Desire 11, 24-25, 36, 40-41, 44, 63, 69-70, 73, 77, 128, 148, 156,
159, 167, 187, 227. 258, 262,
Destiny 79, 89, 125, 128. 135, 192, 284, 287
Dilts, Robert 290
Distortion 43
Dreams 5, 7, 9, 12, 16, 24, 63, 70, 128-129, 134, 144, 158, 231, 259,
269, 281-284

E

Ecological 146-147, 149
Energy Direction 56, 95, 126
Expanded Awareness 106-108, 110-112, 247

F

Filters 46, 99, 285
Filtration Process 42
Finances 70
Future 137, 144-145, 149-151, 154

G

Game 3, 10-11, 20, 22, 24-26, 29, 39-40, 44-47, 49, 75, 81-82,
    86-87, 101, 106-107, 129-130, 135, 144, 166, 267-268, 290
Generalization 44, 239
Genius Reading 106, 110-111
Goals 3, 137, 140

H

Hypnosis 8, 289

I

Imagination 152
Influence 3, 185, 227, 289
Integrity 140, 200, 261, 291
Intention 241

L

Language 50, 61, 99, 116, 126, 233
Leadership 55, 94, 126, 227, 281, 284-285

M

Master 90, 100, 167, 185, 242, 285-286
Meta Model 217, 219
Meta Programs 51, 52, 61, 68, 90, 99, 110, 125, 285
Mind Mapping 110, 114-117, 124
Mission 3, 137, 139, 141, 143, 292
Modeling 77, 79, 81-82
Motivation 52, 90, 125

N

Navigate 128, 135, 144, 151, 154, 255, 283
Negotiating 212, 220, 222, 249, 290
Neurological Repatterning™ 285
Neuro Linguistic Programming 8, 218
Neurology 113, 117

O

Orientation 53, 92, 126

Outcome 17, 30, 48, 137, 139, 145, 147-149, 155-156, 160-161, 173, 175, 200, 213, 216-217, 221-223, 227, 229, 251, 258, 287

P

Perception 15, 25, 30, 33, 35, 49, 65, 90, 195, 233-235, 238, 241, 260, 277-278

Performance 56, 95, 126, 287, 287

Physiology 163, 172, 175

Playing Field 3, 10, 19-20, 22-23, 25-26, 49, 51, 78, 82, 128, 135, 137-138, 144, 151, 157, 167, 268

Potentiality 19-20, 138

Power 3, 5, 9, 11, 78, 167, 171, 187, 227, 230, 283, 285, 287, 290, 292

Preferred Interest 57, 96, 126

Principles 227

Projection 65

Pure Potentiality 19-20, 138

Purpose 244

R

Rapport 3, 171, 173-174, 176, 184, 202, 207

Reality 29, 33, 46

Reciprocity 227

Representational System 178-180, 182

Results 281

Reticular Activating System 41, 111

S

Sales 3, 127, 199, 288

Sensory Acuity 167

Speed Modeling™ 3, 8-9, 75, 85, 105-106, 110, 282

Spin Patterns 235, 237, 242

Story 3, 233, 249, 251

Strategic Visioning™ 144-145, 148, 151, 154, 158-159, 283

Success 3, 11, 54, 92, 126, 137, 159, 161, 188, 241, 255, 283, 285, 288-289

T

Team 3, 5, 57, 96, 165-166, 197
Time Awareness 60, 99, 126
Time Stream 151-154, 156-157, 159
Traits 101, 127
Trump, Donald 292

V

Values 3, 46, 61, 68-69, 88, 119, 124, 137, 139, 185-193, 195-196,
 237, 285
Vision 3, 137-139, 141-142

W

Wealth 5, 9-10, 78, 167, 283, 285, 287-290
Win-Win Selling Process 201
Work Satisfaction 57, 96, 126